RAILROADS

RAILROADS

THE HISTORY OF THE AMERICAN RAILROADS IN 500 PHOTOS

Steve Barry

This edition first published in 2002 by Crestline, an imprint of
MBI Publishing Company, Galtier Plaza, Suite 200,
380 Jackson Street, St. Paul, MN 55101-3885 USA

The information in this book is true and complete to the best
of our knowledge. All recommendations are made without any
guarantee on the part of the author or Publisher, who also
disclaim any liability incurred in connection with the use of
this data or specific details.

We recognize that some words, model names and
designations, for example, mentioned herein are the property
of the trademark holder. We use them for identification
purposes only. This is not an official publication.

MBI Publishing Company books are also available at discounts
in bulk quantity for industrial or sales-promotional use. For
details write to Special Sales Manager at Motorbooks
International Wholesalers & Distributors, Galtier Plaza, Suite
200, 380 Jackson Street, St. Paul, MN 55101-3885 USA.

Library of Congress Cataloging-in-Publication Data Available

ISBN 0-7603-1438-1

Designed and edited by:
FOCUS PUBLISHING, 11a St Botolph's Road, Sevenoaks,
Kent, England TN13 3AJ
Editors: Guy Croton, Vanessa Townsend
Designer: David Etherington

Salamander editor: Marie Clayton
Salamander publishing director: Colin Gower

Printed and bound in Taiwan

Contents

Introduction

Perhaps no two histories are as intertwined as those of the United States (and its neighbor to the north, Canada), and railroads. It was the railroads that took a young agricultural nation and helped it become a manufacturing and economic powerhouse. The building of the transcontinental railroad is one of the most fabled events in US history. Indeed, a transcontinental railroad was deemed so important in Canada, that British Columbia wouldn't join the confederation of provinces without a guarantee that rails would eventually stretch across the country. It was railroads that provided the key transportation arteries that allowed the Union to defeat the southern uprising in the Civil War, and it was railroads that moved munitions and troops across the continent in two world wars.

We are fortunate that so much of the history of railroads was captured in the various art media throughout time, for it provides a look at a growing continent. From railroad art work promoting new trains that were conquering the frontiers, to line drawings of early locomotives, we see the first half of the 19th century. And when the camera came along, many photographers turned their talents to capturing the rail scene. Railroads and North America are indeed an inseparable combination.

Right: The peacefulness of the Canadian prairie at sunset is reflected in the rails at Mortlach, Saskatchewan, along Canadian Pacific's main line.

Opposite: Main line railroad movements are governed by signals, none more stately than the semaphore type such as this one near Paradise, Montana.

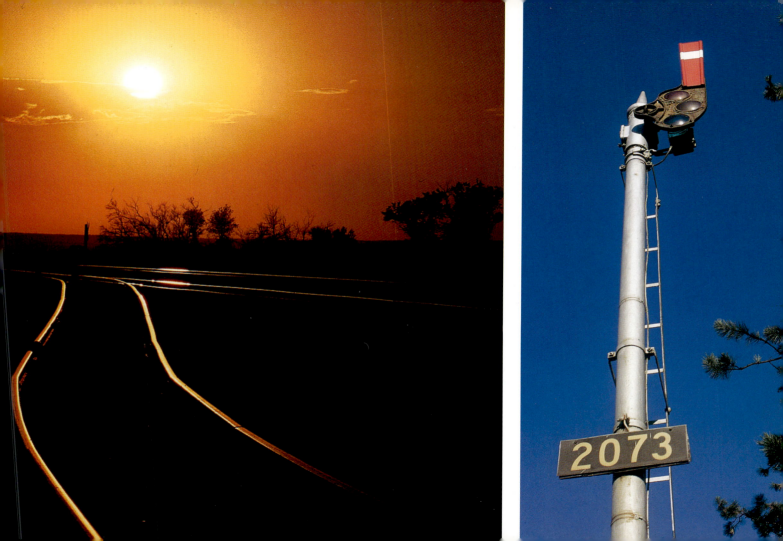

1

History: Rails West!

The story of North America's railroads is the story of the development of the countries of the United States and Canada. Growth for both countries exploded in the 1800s, when reliable rail service united cities on the east and west coasts with reliable transportation. Indeed, the western provinces of Canada wouldn't join the confederation without a transcontinental railroad. The railroads took North America from an agricultural society into an economic powerhouse.

Left: A typical passenger train from the 1890s meets a typical passenger train from the 1990s along the Strasburg Rail Road in Pennsylvania.

The First American Railroads

To define "one moment" that gave birth to railroading would be almost impossible. Diverse influences, from the Egyptians to French inventors, all contributed to what we now know as railroads. After all, when the pyramids were built, the Egyptians discovered that moving the heavy stones on rollers on a firm roadway made the work easier. And it was Nicolas-Joseph Cugnot who invented a steam-powered carriage in France in 1769. And prior to Cugnot, Thomas Newcomen was the first to patent a steam engine design, doing so in 1705. And developments were made in steam-powered ships before anyone thought of propelling a railroad train by steam. And the idea of a railroad—carriages operating on a fixed guideway—came from England in 1630, where coal was transported over wooden planks.

Below: Colonel John Stevens ran this crude rack steam locomotive in his back yard in Hoboken, New Jersey, in 1825.

The first railroad in the United States was built in Quincy, Massachusetts, in 1827 to haul granite from quarries to the river. A coal-hauling railroad was built in Pennsylvania in 1827. But these used horses for power. The Delaware & Hudson Canal Company's railroad, built in 1828, was the first to try steam power when it purchased the Stourbridge Lion from Foster & Rastrick in England in 1829. On August 8 of that year, the Lion made its first run in Honesdale, Pennsylvania. Railroads had arrived.

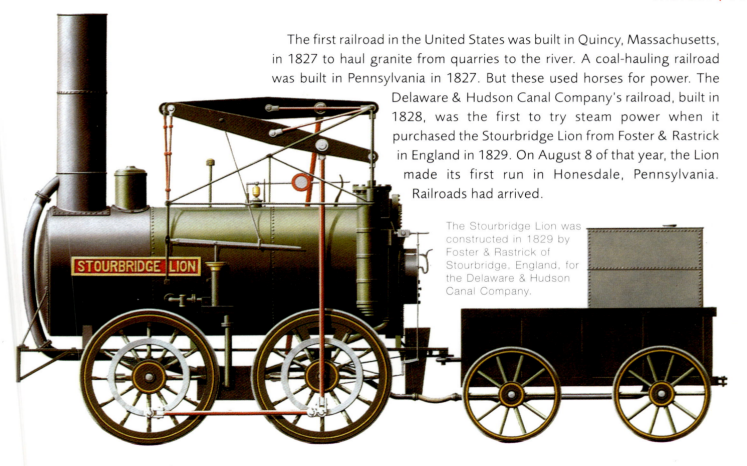

The Stourbridge Lion was constructed in 1829 by Foster & Rastrick of Stourbridge, England, for the Delaware & Hudson Canal Company.

Steam Proves its Worth

Left: The Tom Thumb was challenged to a race with a horse in 1830. A broken belt caused the Thumb to lose the race, but it had proven its superiority.

Below: The Tom Thumb pulls a typical coach of the 1830s. With only two axles, it's certain that it wasn't a smooth ride. A replica of the Tom Thumb operates at the B&O Railroad Museum.

The Baltimore & Ohio Railroad built its line from Baltimore westward 13 miles to Ellicott City, Maryland, starting on July 4, 1828. A steam locomotive was ordered from England, but was damaged in transit. Even though sceptics thought that a steam locomotive could not travel on the B&O's many curves along the Patapsco River, Peter Cooper designed the Tom Thumb. On August 28, 1830, the Tom Thumb merrily steamed the entire distance without incident.

PETER COOPER'S "TOM THUMB" 1829-30 BALTIMORE & OHIO R.R.

The John Bull

The seeds of what would become the mighty Pennsylvania Railroad were planted in New Jersey in the 1830s. The Camden & Amboy, running between Camden (across from Philadelphia) and South Amboy (across from New York City), began using steam power when the John Bull entered service in 1831.

The locomotive arrived from England unassembled and without instructions. The C&A's master mechanic, Isaac Dripps, assembled the locomotive and added items that would become standards on nearly all American locomotives for the next 150 years. Dripps was the first to mount a headlight, bell, and pilot (cowcatcher) to a locomotive.

Below: The John Bull was constructed in 1831 for the Camden & Amboy Railroad (an early predecessor of the Pennsylvania Railroad) by George and Robert Stephenson of England. It was shipped to the United States in pieces and assembled by Isaac Dripps of the C&A, who added a bell and headlight.

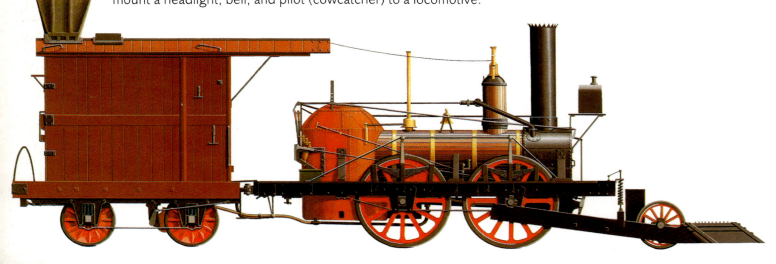

Left: The John Bull was fitted with many accessories that would soon become standard on locomotives, such as a headlight, bell, and cab.

Below: The Camden & Amboy Railroad used the John Bull to power passenger trains across New Jersey in the 1830s. The original John Bull still exists.

Left: An operating replica of the John Bull built by the Pennsylvania Railroad in 1940 gives insight into how an engineer from the 1830s would view the railroad.

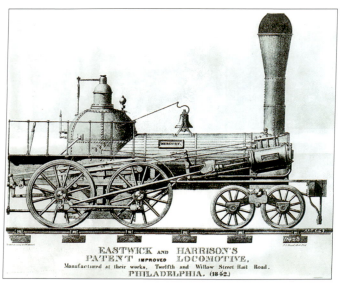

EASTWICK AND HARRISON'S
PATENT IMPROVED LOCOMOTIVE,
Manufactured at their works, Twelfth and Willow Street Rail Road.
PHILADELPHIA. (1842.)

Above: Locomotive builder Eastwick & Harrison issued this lithograph advertising their services to the fledgling rail industry.

Further Development

The railroad industry at the start of the 1840s hardly resembled what it was at the start of the 1830s. Mileage had grown from less than 100 to nearly 3,000 and locomotives were already getting more powerful. In addition to the Camden &

It didn't take long for coaches to get fancier. The bottom part of the coach probably offered a fair ride, but the riders up top had to deal with hot ash.

Amboy, Baltimore & Ohio, and Delaware & Hudson, steam railroads were sprouting up in South Carolina and elsewhere. Developments in railroad technology were also occurring, some of which would become permanent features of railroading into the 21st Century. The four-wheel truck became standard. Steam locomotives had pilot wheels added to help negotiate curves. Signals were invented to control train movements, as was the timetable. The canal companies, who started building about the same time as the railroads, never had a chance. Railroads had quickly become the transportation choice.

Steam Locomotive Development

Steam locomotive design made quantum improvements during the 1830s. While the early locomotives resembled sewing machines run amok, development soon gave a familiar look to the smoking beasts. Boilers were placed horizontally on the frame, and the driving wheels were connected by rods to horizontal cylinders at the front of the locomotive. Smoke stacks, while usually large, were nonetheless mounted in the familiar spot at the front of the locomotive, and the engineer and fireman were removed from platforms next to the boiler and placed in a cab at the rear of the locomotive. Tenders for carrying water and fuel (wood or coal) were added. In just a very short time, locomotive development had come a long, long way.

Below: The Pioneer operated on the Cumberland Valley, a subsidiary of the Pennsylvania Railroad.

Right: A replica of the Lafayette of the Baltimore & Ohio now operates at the B&O Railroad Museum. The original was built in 1837.

Building the Railroads

The earliest railroads consisted of wooden rails mounted on stone "sleepers" with an iron strap on top of the rail. Soon the stone sleepers were replaced by wooden crossties, still a common practice, although some railroads now use concrete ties. But the "strap rail" remained for a few more years, with one deadly flaw—as the nails that held the iron strap to the wooden rails wore away, the strap would let loose and come flying through the floors of the coaches, sometimes with deadly results. The solution was to use rails made entirely of iron. But when the US railroads went to iron rail, they imported it from England because it was less expensive than US-produced iron and was of a higher quality. Robert Stevens is attributed with inventing the modern rail, a piece of iron rolled into a "T" shape. The top could support the weight of a train, while the bottom could be spiked directly to the wooden ties. Soon all railroads were using imported "T" rail.

Below: Some of the instruments used to build the Baltimore & Ohio included a custom-made shovel and axe used to make the first dig in the construction project, a surveyor's compass and chain, plans, stock certificates (you can't build without money), and even masonic sashes worn at the opening ceremony for the railroad.

Below: The 0-8-0 "Mud-digger" Class of locomotives, the first to have a horizontal boiler, were developed by Ross Winans of the Baltimore & Ohio.

But even though a standard rail was now being used, the distance between the rails was still varying from railroad to railroad. Gauges varied from railroad to railroad, and most railroads decided on which gauge to use based on the gauge of the locomotives it first purchased. The Delaware & Hudson built to 4ft 3in gauge to accommodate the Stourbridge Lion. Gauges varied to as wide as 6ft. It was the eastern roads that first began to standardize on the 4ft 8$\frac{1}{2}$in that is used today, although there were notable exceptions such as the Erie and the Lackawanna, at 6ft.

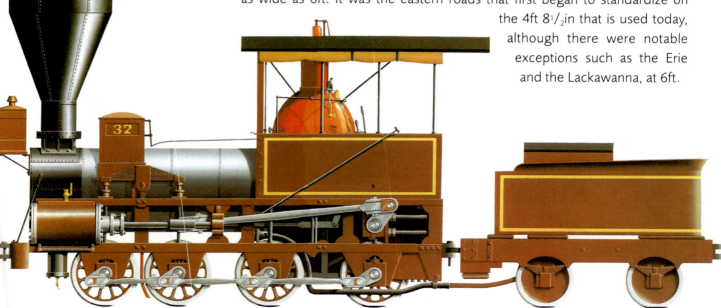

Above: The "American"-type 4-4-0 locomotive was developed by the Rogers Locomotive Works in the mid-19th Century.

Below: Production of "Consolidation"-type 2-8-0 locomotives began in 1866. By 1946 over 24,000 of the freight locomotives had been produced.

Fine Locomotives and Cars

By the 1850s, a standard locomotive was coming into favor—the 4-4-0 "American" type (although the system that would classify it as a 4-4-0 and call it an "American" type wouldn't be invented until 1901). Meanwhile, passenger travel was getting more plush. While the travelers of the 1830s had to be content with riding on two-axle flat cars with benches, the invention of the two-axle truck (with a truck at each end of a coach, for four axles total) allowed longer cars with a better ride. As more and more railroads came into being, competition grew as more than one railroad would cover the same route. That meant railroads were soon engaged in a war to attract passengers, and they used amenities like plush seats, food service, and the like to draw in patrons.

Right: The invention of the four-wheel truck and the application of two of these to a passenger car (one at each end) allowed coaches to become longer and more spacious, as well as more comfortable and posh.

America's Locomotive

For the 1850s and 1860s, the 4-4-0 locomotive was the pinnacle of steam development. A variety of locomotive builders were making them, and a railroad could buy an "off-the-shelf" model and add a few options as it saw fit. Most railroads were decorating their locomotives with bright paint and sparkling trim, and many locomotives received names (in fact, three of the most famous named locomotives in US history—the General, the Texas, and the Jupiter—were all 4-4-0s). It was indeed a colorful era on the rails. The 4-4-0 was significant in that it spawned the next generation of locomotives. The 4-4-0s were stretched into 4-6-0 "Ten-Wheelers," which gave rise to the 2-8-0 "Consolidation"-type, the first locomotive destined for primarily freight service.

Left: An advertising poster extolled the virtues of riding from Chicago to St. Paul through Wisconsin by train. The only other way was via the Great Lakes on a ship.

Right: The William Crooks was the first locomotive to operate west of the Mississippi River when it entered service in Minnesota. It was a typical 4-4-0 of the period.

The US Civil War (or "The War Between the States" as it is often called) from 1861–65 was the first where railroads played a significant role. They moved materials and troops from one location to another rapidly, and some say the Union's superior rail network had much to do with its eventual victory over the Confederacy. Destroying the railroads was a primary goal during the war, and rebuilding them was a primary goal after the war.

Below: The General became the most famous locomotive of the 19th Century when it was stolen by Union spies during the Civil War.

Below: The General Haupt was built by manufacturer William Mason in 1863. During the war, virtually all the main line locomotives were 4-4-0s.

One of the most famous incidents of the Civil War occurred on April 25, 1862, when a group of 20 Union spies led by James J. Andrews stole the 4-4-0 General at Big Shanty, Georgia, and set out to cripple the Western & Atlantic Railroad, a major artery for the Confederacy, by burning 15 bridges between Big Shanty and Chattanooga. But once the theft was made, the train's conductor, William Fuller, set out chasing the stolen train, first on foot and ultimately by using the 4-4-0 Texas. Fuller disrupted Andrews' plans, and the raid failed.

Coast to Coast

It soon became clear that a transcontinental rail route was needed to unite California with the rest of the United States. President Abraham Lincoln signed the Pacific Railroad Act on July 1, 1862, during the Civil War. The Union Pacific began building westward across Nebraska, while the Central Pacific started building from California in 1866. No one knew where the two lines would actually meet. Under the direction of Major General Grenville M. Dodge, the UP steadily proceeded with laborers from Ireland who had come to the US to escape their homeland famine. Out west, the Central Pacific had a much more formidable challenge in the Sierra Nevada mountains, but construction superintendent J.H. Strobridge found that his Chinese laborers were more than up to the task. The UP encountered miles of endless prairies with no trees to use for crossties, while everything the CP needed had to be shipped around Cape Horn to California.

Below: Straight out of the old west, a 4-4-0 stops at Wyoming Station in 1868, one year before the completion of the transcontinental railroad. Note the antlers on the headlight.

Opposite: Probably the most famous railroad photograph ever was this one taken on May 10, 1869, at Promontory, Utah. The gold spike had just been driven in by California Governor Leland Stanford, and for the first time in its history the United States was joined coast-to-coast by a railroad. The Union Pacific built from the east and the Central Pacific built from the west. The CP soon became the Southern Pacific.

Done!

The transcontinental railroad that had been started in 1866 was nearing completion three years later as the Union Pacific and Central Pacific converged in the Utah desert north of the Great Salt Lake. Because no definite meeting point had been set, the two railroads actually passed each other at one point, working on grading but never laying tracks. Finally, Promontory, Utah, was set as the meeting point, and a Central Pacific train behind the Jupiter headed from Sacramento, while a Union Pacific train from Omaha headed west behind 4-4-0 No.119. As the two trains approached the final gap in the transcontinental railroad, a laurel crosstie was placed at the meeting spot. Silver spikes from Nevada, Idaho, and Montana were provided, as was a gold spike from California. Wires were connected to the final spike so telegraphs across the country would receive the actual driving of the spike by California Governor Leland Stanford. Once the work was complete, the telegraph tapped out a single word—"Done!"

Below: The site of the driving of the golden spike is now a US National Historic Site. Replicas of the Jupiter and No.119 touch pilots several times each day in a recreation of the event.

Right: It's time to pay the workers. The pay train pauses in Hays, Kansas, sometime during the 1870s or 1880s. These cash-laden trains became the target for train robbers, at least in the movies.

Below: The Jupiter is a typical example of the "American"-type 4-4-0 locomotives that dominated railroad motive power for most of the last part of the 19th Century.

More Rails

The driving of the gold spike (along with the end of the Civil War) started a building boom in the railroad industry, which was just barely a half century old. Rail mileage in the US stood at 35,000 at the end of the war, but had swelled to 156,000 by 1888. The second transcontinental railroad, the Northern Pacific, was completed in 1883. The Santa Fe and Great Northern soon had transcontinental routes as well. The railroads of the east were becoming the financial toys of people like Jay Gould and Cornelius Vanderbilt. The railroads were also becoming the largest employer in the country and their economic impact was widespread as they were consumers of material like iron as well as the primary shipper for goods from coast to coast. By 1880 the nation was dependent on railroads as the sole viable transportation form, a status the railroads would enjoy for the next 30 years. Almost every piece of the country with a farm or a mine had a railroad nearby—it had become not a luxury, but a necessity.

Above: Railroads developed ornate heralds, as the print media was their only advertising outlet.

Opposite: To serve lightly-used passenger lines, the Rio Grande Southern used converted trucks which the railroad dubbed "Galloping Geese."

Right: The Union Pacific advertised that you could get from Nebraska to California in only four and a half days, riding overnight in sleeping cars.

Locomotive Builders

While a number of locomotive builders were formed during the early years of railroad expansion, the American Locomotive Company united eight small builders into one conglomerate in 1901. With an erecting shop that covered over 100 acres in Schenectady, New York, American became one of the two largest steam builders in the country. The other was the Baldwin Locomotive Works of Philadelphia (and later Eddystone), Pennsylvania. Formed by Matthias William Baldwin, the company started designing steam locomotives in the 1830s and by 1870 Baldwin was the largest builder. There were other smaller builders such as the Lima Locomotive Works of Lima, Ohio, which was most famous for producing "super" steam locomotives such as Nickel Plate's 2-8-4 Berkshires and Southern Pacific's Daylight 4-8-4s, as well as Shay geared logging locomotives. Some railroads such as the Pennsylvania and the Norfolk & Western built their own steam power. Baldwin stopped building steam in 1948, and one year later American and Lima also stopped.

Left: Each locomotive builder attached a "builder's plate" to every locomotive produced (bottom row). They also issued catalogs (right) and operating guides (left). Baldwin was established in 1831 and American was formed in 1901 by merging several smaller companies. These would become the dominant manufacturers in the early part of the 20th Century, although Lima also started building in 1916. Although all three built diesels as well, none would survive beyond the 1970s.

Above: To stabilize its Lucin Cut-Off across the Great Salt Lake, the Southern Pacific dumped several old freight carts into the salty water.

Industrial Monuments

Some of the greatest construction works were produced by railroads, usually without government or public funding. The Central Pacific's crossing of the Sierra Nevada during the building of the transcontinental railroad certainly is one of the most ambitious projects ever encountered, but there were many others that were just as spectacular. Looking to trim 100 miles off its route to California, the Southern Pacific decided to build across the Great Salt Lake rather than go around it, and on Thanksgiving Day 1903 the Lucin Cut-Off was officially opened. The Delaware, Lackawanna & Western modernized its line across eastern Pennsylvania with several magnificent concrete viaducts and pushed across New Jersey on its own Cut-Off. The Hell Gate Bridge, linking Manhattan with lower New England, was opened in 1917. The bridge and associated

approaches are almost ten miles long. Another famous bridge is the Rockville Bridge in Pennsylvania, which is the longest stone arch bridge in the world. The projects taken on by the railroads were huge, even by today's standards, and they were built to last. Most of the great construction projects of the late 19th and early 20th Centuries are still in use.

Left: As the railroads expanded westward, commerce moved in along the tracks. All across the prairies grain elevators sprouted like the wheat they stored. Once a common sight, the wooden grain elevator became a victim of economics, replaced by modern high-capacity concrete silos.

Below: One of the engineering marvels in the eastern United States was the main line of the Delaware, Lackawanna & Western, which built four large concrete viaducts in 1903, the largest at Nicholson, Pennsylvania.

Standardization

While every railroad had its own way of doing things during the first 60 years of railroading, the growth of the industry meant that railroads had to interact with each other. And to successfully accomplish that, railroads needed to standardize. One of the ways they standardized was in the way time was kept—every town had its own time based on the sun, but trains were moving from town to town. How could a train crew keep track of time when they might encounter a dozen different "time zones?" The solution came from the American Railway Association at a meeting in 1883. At that meeting, it was determined that all US railroads would keep time based on four time zones. And since the economies and transportation in most US cities relied on the railroads, the towns adopted railroad time. The US Congress officially adopted railroad time as the US standard in 1918. Standardization also came in motive power, as the major builders switched production to diesel locomotives. Railroads were now able to buy locomotives out of a catalog, just like buying a car.

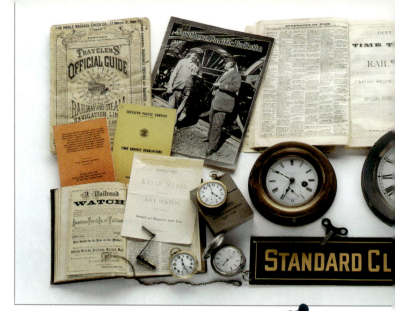

Left: To control the movements of trains, railroads developed timetables that established where trains should be at a given time. With no way of communicating with each other, strict timekeeping was the only way to avoid collisions. Crew members carried precise watches, and these were checked against a master clock at each division point and among the crew during the run. With most of the US basing timekeeping on the sun (straight up was noon), the railroads were forced to establish four time zones across the US to keep from having to deal with numerous "local times."

Right: The famous Hell Gate Bridge was built by the New York, New Haven & Hartford to bring electric trains into New York City starting in 1917. The bridge is still used today by Amtrak.

Left: The diesel that felled the steam locomotive was FT No.103 built by General Motors in 1939, which went on a 20 railroad demonstration tour.

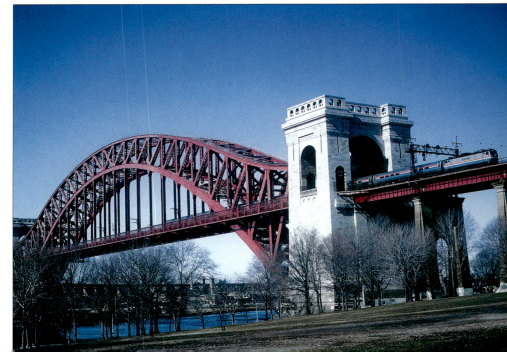

Above: Canadian National staged this publicity photo that demonstrated the development of the railroad's motive power from early steam to diesel.

Right: The New York, Ontario & Western became the first major US railroad to completely abandon its entire line following bankruptcy, doing so in 1957.

Left: The US railroads were stretched to capacity during the Second World War, as men and machinery were dispatched across the nation.

Boom and Bust

The US railroads hit their apex as the country entered the Second World War. During the First World War, the railroads had been nationalized, but the government didn't feel it was necessary in 1941. Thus, the railroads operated independently, although the government placed restrictions on locomotive purchases. But the railroads certainly moved some tonnage during 1941–45. Constant parades of troop trains heading for the west coast and army material moving everywhere put the railroads at capacity.

It was probably the finest hour for the industry. Unfortunately, the boom of World War II didn't last. Shortly after the end of the war, the jet passenger airliner was perfected and the US ambitiously built highways. With passengers leaving for the air or the automobile and more and more freight moving by truck, the railroads hit hard times. No one knew just how hard until the New York, Ontario & Western became the first railroad to simply abandon its entire line, doing so in 1957.

Hitting the Bottom

The troubles of the late 1950s only deepened in the 1960s. Two bitter rivals, the New York Central and the Pennsylvania Railroad, merged in 1967 to form Penn Central. But Penn Central itself was a monumental failure, filing for bankruptcy in 1970. This event led to a near-collapse of all northeast railroads, as one by one the Jersey Central, Erie Lackawanna, Reading, Lehigh Valley, and others followed Penn Central into bankruptcy. The western railroads were staying alive, but the good times were over. The passenger train was a money-losing proposition all across the country, and on May 1, 1971, Amtrak was formed to take over all intercity passenger operations. Literally overnight, the number of passenger trains was cut in half. The government stepped in again and formed Conrail in 1976, combining most of the bankrupt eastern roads into one system. As the US celebrated its bicentennial in 1976, railroading was at its lowest point. Nonetheless, the railroads still hosted the American Freedom Train for the US milestone.

Opposite, inset: Passenger rail service in the United States was nationalized in 1971 under the Amtrak name as railroads sought to shed the money-losing trains.

Above: Penn Central was formed by merging the New York Central and Pennsylvania Railroads in 1967. By 1973 the PC was bankrupt.

Opposite: During 1975 and 1976 the steam-powered American Freedom Train toured the United States, celebrating the nation's bicentennial.

End of a Golden Age?

The railroads certainly have had a colorful history. During the 1980s, reminders of its Golden Age (generally regarded as 1900–1945 or so) were vanishing. The great passenger stations were closing down and the remnants of the infrastructure built for steam was crumbling. Amtrak still ran passenger trains, but they couldn't compare to the great streamliners of the 1940s. But a transformation occurred in the late 1980s. New traffic was found, the railroads were able to shed unprofitable lines (which the government wouldn't allow up to that point), and passenger trains entered a new high-speed era in the Northeast. At the dawn of the 21st Century, it's good times again for North America's railroads.

Above: Some 50 years after diesels vanquished steam from the railroad scene, reminders of the steam era such as this water tank could be found.

Opposite: The Broadway Limited celebrated its 80th anniversary in 1986, with a celebration featuring trains from 1906 and 1986.

Left: Once common in big city terminals, the last train shed in the US was Reading Terminal in Philadelphia, which was closed in 1984.

2

Steam Freight Trains

Perhaps no technological development had as much immediate impact on the United States economy as the development of the steam locomotive. By the late 1850s, freight could be moved rapidly across the east, and by the 1860s could be moved all the way across the country, opening new markets for producers.

Left: A typical freight train from the 1930s is recreated on the Strasburg Rail Road in 1994 for the benefit of railroad enthusiasts.

Above: Steam locomotives were taken to the roundhouse for quick repairs and servicing between runs. This roundhouse was at Armstrong, Kansas.

Left: A trim 4-4-0 sporting a tall smokestack leads the first grain train on the Chicago, Rock Island & Pacific at Hebron, Nebraska, in 1887.

Below: The Manitou & Pikes Peak Railway developed rack locomotives to ascend to the top of the famous mountain in Colorado. The boiler was inclined to keep water level while the locomotive was negotiating the line's steep hills.

Above: A train crew poses in front of their caboose on the Union Pacific at Grand Island, Nebraska, in 1898. Cabooses were a staple at the end of freight trains until the mid-1980s.

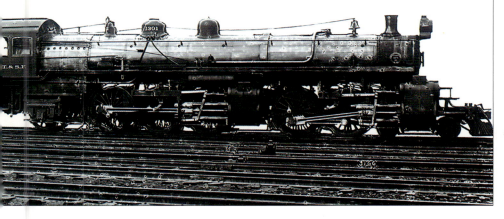

Left: An early attempt at "articulation" (two sets of drivers powered by independent cylinders) was this 4-4-6-2 built for the Santa Fe. Most articulateds that followed had an equal number of drivers working from each cylinder set.

Below: Nevada-California-Oregon No.9 was built in 1909 for freight service on narrow gauge tracks in California. The semi-circular tender held water and oil.

Opposite: An American-type 4-4-0 locomotive leads a freight train on the Wilmington & Western in Delaware during a rail photo charter. The first car in the train is a "wagon-roof" boxcar, which were used by the Baltimore & Ohio Railroad.

Left: A policeman keeps a careful eye on bananas being unloaded for agricultural inspectors at Baltimore, Maryland, in 1910. The coming of the railroads meant produce could be shipped anywhere in the country, no matter where it was grown.

When the Denver & Rio Grande's narrow gauge empire was expanding through the Rocky Mountains in the latter part of the 19th Century, it became obvious that stronger locomotives than the 4-4-0s and 2-6-0s then operating were needed. In 1877, Baldwin supplied the D&RG with its first 2-8-0, numbered 22 and named Alamosa. This was the first of what would become a fleet of 130 Consolidations, most in the C-16 Class but a few in the longer C-19 Class. These locomotives were the workhorses for the D&RG until the main line became standard gauge in 1889–90.

DENVER & RIO GRANDE

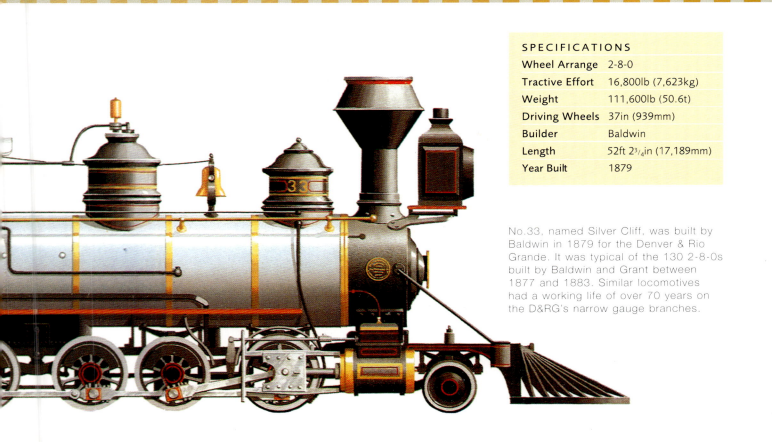

SPECIFICATIONS

Wheel Arrange	2-8-0
Tractive Effort	16,800lb (7,623kg)
Weight	111,600lb (50.6t)
Driving Wheels	37in (939mm)
Builder	Baldwin
Length	52ft 2³/₄in (17,189mm)
Year Built	1879

No.33, named Silver Cliff, was built by Baldwin in 1879 for the Denver & Rio Grande. It was typical of the 130 2-8-0s built by Baldwin and Grant between 1877 and 1883. Similar locomotives had a working life of over 70 years on the D&RG's narrow gauge branches.

Left: A string of light Mikados based on the standards of the United States Railroad Administration await their next assignments in 1915. The Mikado was one of the most popular freight locomotive types.

Opposite: The sight of coal smoke was common in small towns and big cities for over a century as all across the nation railroads worked 24 hours a day.

Below: Maine had the largest network of two-foot-gauge railroads in the United States, operated by diminutive locomotives such as No. 7. When the lines were abandoned, No. 7 found a home on the Edaville tourist railroad.

Right: The Shay locomotive was invented by Ephraim Shay as a low-speed high-power locomotive. It used vertical cylinders to power a crankshaft that delivered power to the wheels.

Opposite: Shay locomotives were most commonly used in logging operations where track was quickly laid with little or no grading.

Below: Prairie No.24 of the Sandy River & Rangely Lakes worked the narrow gauge lines of Maine.

Above: In 1920 the cattle and meatpacking center at Omaha, Nebraska, was a busy place. Livestock was hauled in ventilated stock cars, providing a source for fresh meat throughout the US.

Opposite: The Cass Scenic Railroad in West Virginia is the finest example of a preserved logging railroad. Multiple Shay locomotives now haul passengers instead of logs on Bald Knob.

Below: Tracks were laid into the forests and timber was hauled out, such as in this operation in Washington state around 1925.

Left: East Broad Top No.14 rests inside the line's roundhouse at Orbisonia, Pennsylvania. Once a coal-hauler, the EBT survives hauling tourists.

Far left: The EBT roundhouse and shop complex is the finest example of 1940s-era railroad industry to survive. The railroad ceased carrying freight in 1956.

Opposite: Despite no longer operating as a freight hauler, the EBT can still recreate a bygone era when a photographers' charter is run.

Below: Sandy River & Rangeley Lakes No.24 was built by Baldwin in 1919 and retired in 1935 when the railroad was abandoned. Purchased by a rail enthusiast, the locomotive was nevertheless eventually scrapped.

With traffic during World War I straining capacity, the coal-hauling Virginian Railroad needed something that could lug heavy trains uphill. Despite the failure of most articulated locomotives with more than 16 driving wheels, the railroad turned to the American Locomotive Company and ordered several 2-10-10-2s in 1918. Sporting four-foot diameter low pressure cylinders, the largest ever used on a steam locomotive, the "800s" were a surprising success, serving the railroad faithfully into the 1940s. They were likely the most successful locomotive with 20 driving wheels ever built.

SPECIFICATIONS

Wheel Arrange	2-10-10-2	Driving Wheels	56in (1,422mm)
Tractive Effort	176,600lb (80,127kg)	Builder	American Locomotive
Weight	898,000lb (407.4t)	Length	99ft 8in (30,368mm)
		Year Built	1918

Below: Articulated "mallets" were used on extra heavy trains. The locomotives had both high-pressure and low-pressure cylinders. The Virginian used the 800 Class 2-10-10-2s to push heavy coal trains out of the West Virginia mountains.

Above: The heaviest power used on the Denver & Rio Grande's narrow gauge lines in Colorado were 2-8-2s. No.487 was built by Baldwin in 1925.

Opposite: Union Pacific No.618, a "Consolidation"-type 2-8-0, pulls a train of tank cars. The 618 was built in 1907.

Above: The most famous triplex ever constructed was the Erie's 2-8-8-8-2. It was less than a success.

Left: The White Pass & Yukon Route relied on 2-8-2s built by Baldwin to operate the narrow gauge line from Skagway, Alaska, into Yukon Territory.

Opposite: To tap the rich silver mining regions of Colorado, the Denver & Rio Grande built narrow gauge tracks (three feet between the rails) into the Rocky Mountains. For most of the 20th Century the Rio Grande relied on a fleet of "Mikado"-type 2-8-2 locomotives built by Baldwin. Many of these locomotives survive today.

Left: The Durango & Silverton Narrow Gauge Railroad operates the former Silverton Branch of the Denver & Rio Grande. Occasionally the railroad operates vintage trains for the benefit of photographers, to recreate narrow gauge railroading of the 1950s.

Opposite: The "high line" near Rockwood, Colorado, is one of the most rugged locations on the Colorado narrow gauge. The Animas River lies 300ft below in the valley. Tourists still ride on this section of track.

Above: Stock cars were used on the narrow gauge lines in Colorado to haul livestock through the Rocky Mountains. Horses and other animals were used for mining, and later cattle were brought in to graze on the grasslands located in valleys beneath the tall mountains.

Right: A typical narrow gauge train would include a boxcar for general freight, tank cars for hauling oil, and stock cars for carrying livestock.

Very few railroads ever attempted using locomotives with 12 driving wheels coupled together, but the Union Pacific, the railroad that always seemed to have the "biggest," ordered 88 4-12-2s from American Locomotive between 1926 and 1930. With more speed than a Mallet, but with similar pulling characteristics, these locomotives were successes in every sense. These locomotives featured a third cylinder mounted under the smokebox between the two outside conventionally-mounted cylinders for extra power.

Below: Union Pacific No.9000 was the first 4-12-2 ordered from American Locomotive by the railroad, delivered in 1926. Sister locomotive 9004 is the only 4-12-2 preserved.

SPECIFICATIONS

Wheel Arrange	4-12-2	Driving Wheels	67in (1,701mm)
Tractive Effort	96,650lb (43,852kg)	Builder	American Locomotive
Weight	782,000lb (354.8t)	Length	102ft 7in (31,267mm)
		Year Built	1926

Above: The Buffalo Creek & Gauley hauled coal from mines in the West Virginia mountains. The railroad used a small fleet of 2-8-0 Consolidations such as No.4, which was built by the Baldwin Locomotive Works in 1926.

Left: Small "tank" engines were used where space was at a premium and operations were confined in a small area. Water was carried in a tank above the boiler rather than in a tender behind the locomotive, while coal was carried in a small bunker.

Below: Union Pacific's 4-12-2 locomotives (9000 Class) had a rugged-looking front end, thanks to the smokebox-mounted air pumps. The third cylinder is visible between the pilot and smokebox.

Above: Due to the severity of the Canadian winters, the Canadian Pacific Railway enclosed its water tanks to provide heat that prevented freezing.

Left: Snow was removed from the right-of-way using plows. Wedge plows such as this were the most common, although some railroads used "rotary" plows.

Above: One of the few users of the 4-8-0 wheel arrangement was the Norfolk & Western, which built many of its own steam locomotives in Roanoke, Virginia.

Left: Consolidation locomotives were
especially suited for hauling freight.
Their short driving wheels meant a lot
of power, but not much speed.

Above: Small diameter driving wheels were especially suitable for mountain railroads where traction was a necessity.

Below: The engineer of Western Maryland No.734 waves to a track inspector in a 1950s scene recreated for photographers on a tourist railroad.

Above: A "Mikado"-type 2-8-2 rides a turntable. The tank over the numbers heated water before it entered the boiler.

Opposite: The Western Maryland Railroad was one of many US lines that hauled coal from the mines.

Left: While steam locomotives could be built to burn either coal or oil, the coalfields of the southern US provided the fuel for all eastern railroads.

Below: Nickel Plate Road No.587 was built by Baldwin in 1918. It was suited for general freight service on the Nickel Plate's lines through Ohio, Indiana, and Pennsylvania.

Left: No.26 served as the plant switcher at the erecting shops of the Baldwin Locomotive Works in Eddystone, Pennsylvania. It is now preserved at Steamtown National Historic Site in Scranton, Pennsylvania.

Above: The Union Railroad had some of the largest switching locomotives ever built. It was unusual for a locomotive with no leading pilot wheels to have ten driving wheels. Baldwin built the Union's 0-10-2s.

The largest steam locomotives to operate in North America were the famed "Big Boy" 4-8-8-4s of the Union Pacific. Designed to haul freight over the Continental Divide at Sherman Hill in Wyoming and across the plains, these locomotives could move a lot of freight at a fairly good speed. The first Big Boy arrived on the UP in late 1941, just in time to help the railroad and the country with the freight moving in the war effort. After the war, the Big Boys were moving perishables across the plains with long strings of orange refrigerator cars trailing. The locomotives remained in service until the late 1950s, and one actually remained in the Cheyenne, Wyoming, roundhouse until the mid-1970s, albeit not serviceable.

SPECIFICATIONS

Wheel Arrange	4-8-8-4	Driving Wheels	68in (1,727mm)
Tractive Effort	135,375lb (61,422kg)	Builder	American Locomotive
Weight	1,189,500lb (539.7t)	Length	132ft 10in (40,487mm)
		Year Built	1941

There are six Big Boy locomotives preserved, but none have operated since being retired by the Union Pacific. But one has to think that someday, just for the sake of doing it, the largest will steam again.

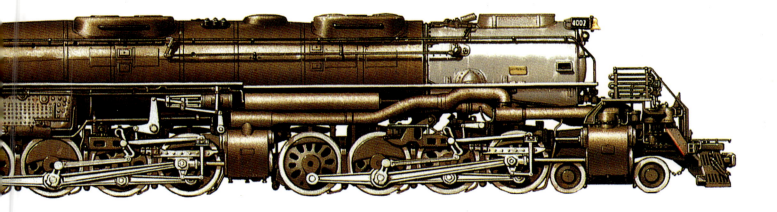

Opposite: Typical freight cars across the years include (clockwise from top left): a wooden boxcar from 1857; a wooden boxcar from 1895; a steel boxcar from 1947; a coal hopper from 1897; another coal hopper from 1880; and another from 1860. In the center is a covered hopper from 1965. Covered hopper cars were used to haul bulk items that could be unloaded by dumping but had to be kept out of the weather, such as grain and cement.

Above: The Duluth, Missabe & Iron Range had mighty 2-8-8-4s to haul ore in Minnesota.

Right: During the Second World War the railroads were vital in the US effort. This poster is from the Union Pacific.

Below: The US Army had several high-drivered (and ungainly looking) Consolidations built for service both in Europe and at home.

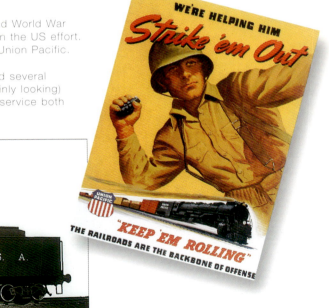

Above: One of the finest examples of articulated steam was the 2-6-6-6 "Allegheny"-types built for the Chesapeake & Ohio. The Lima Locomotive Works built 60 Alleghenys during the 1940s.

Opposite: A "Big Boy" 4-8-8-4 does what it was built to do—haul perishable goods in refrigerated cars at speed over the Continental Divide on Sherman Hill in Wyoming.

Right: "Northern"-type 4-8-4 locomotives were suited for either freight or passenger service. Most roads used them on passenger trains.

Below: The Reading Company's "Northerns" were used exclusively on freight trains. The Reading operated entirely in Pennsylvania.

Left: Steamtown National Historic Site in Scranton, Pennsylvania, has an operating roundhouse where visitors can experience the age of steam.

Above: The conductor gives the "highball" from his modern steel caboose—modern for 1955, the end of the steam era in the United States.

3

Steam Passenger Trains

It wasn't long after the development of the steam locomotive that passengers were soon carried at amazing speeds (over ten miles an hour!) behind the smoking machine. But while the earliest passengers took their lives into their hands riding the rails, the passenger train soon became the most civilized way to travel in the 19th Century.

Left: Three steam locomotives lead a Canadian Pacific passenger train through the Rocky Mountains in British Columbia.

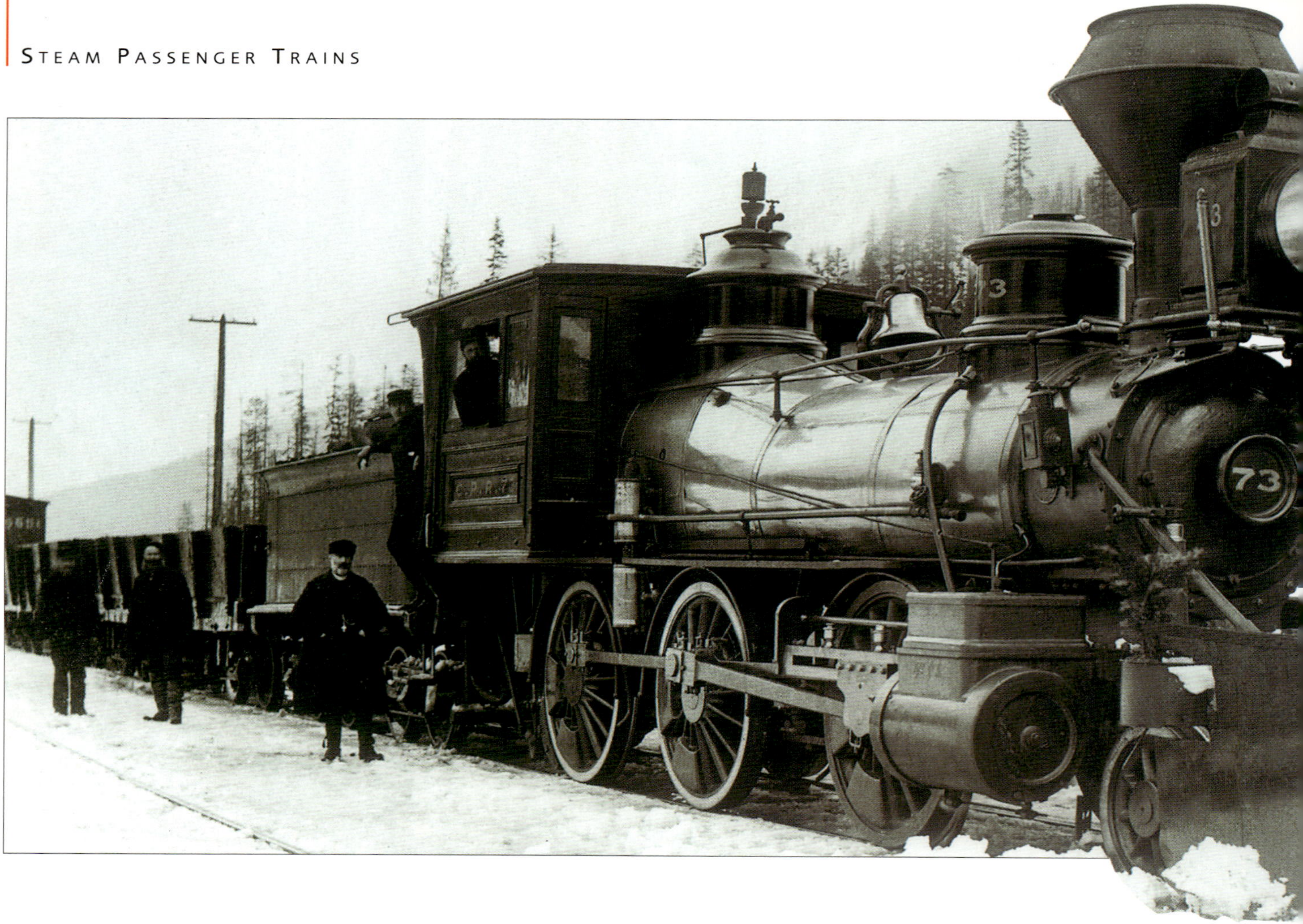
73
73
73

Left: A Canadian Pacific train is at Rogers Pass in the Selkirk Mountains of British Columbia. Leading the train is a 2-6-0. Rogers Pass was the steepest westbound grade on the CPR main line until a new route was constructed through the Mount McDonald Tunnel in the late 1980s.

Above: New York Central No.999 went down in history when it broke all existing speed records by hitting 112.5mph with the Empire State Express on May 10, 1893. The locomotive has been preserved and is on display at the Museum of Science and Industry in Chicago, Illinois.

Right: A "hymn sing" takes place on the Union Pacific Railroad in 1876. On a train, you could do just about anything—sleep, eat, and even go to church.

Above: As railroads introduced new services, they issued colorful brochures touting their superiority over other modes of transportation.

Right: Eureka & Palisade No.4, the Eureka, was built in 1875 by Baldwin for light freight and passenger service on narrow gauge rails.

Left: Early parlor cars were extravagant, with wicker seats, fancy lighting, and polished woodwork.

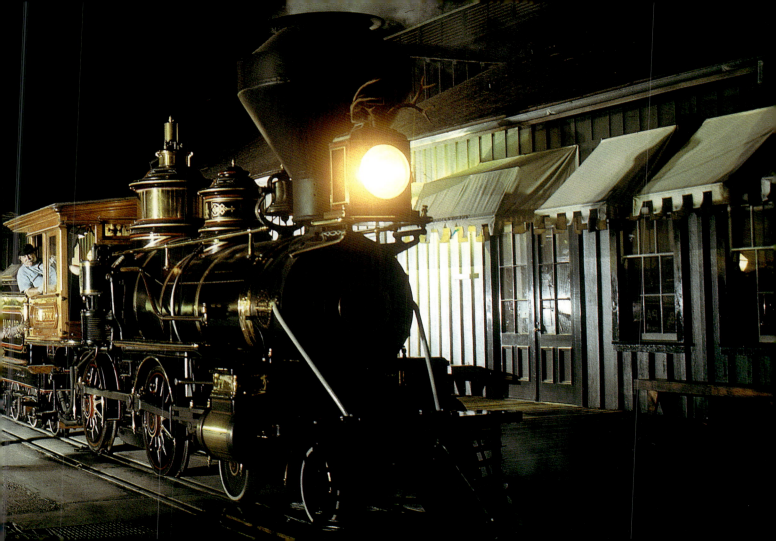

On a stormy night in April 1900, the most famous of all US railroad accidents occurred. The accident, in and of itself, was quite ordinary for the period; it was simply a fast express train striking the rear of a slower freight before the freight had cleared the main line and fully entered a siding. What made the wreck so famous was that it was immortalized in the ballad about the express train's engineer, John Luther "Casey" Jones, who was filling in on the Cannonball Express after finishing his own shift.

SPECIFICATIONS

Wheel Arrange	4-6-0
Tractive Effort	21,930lb (9,950kg)
Weight	205,550lb (93.3t)
Driving Wheels	69in (1,752mm)
Builder	Rogers
Length	60ft 3in (18,364mm)
Year Built	1896

Illinois Central Ten-Wheeler No.382 was the locomotive that Casey Jones was operating on the night of his death. The locomotive was built by the Rogers Locomotive Works of Paterson, New Jersey, in 1896. Repaired and returned to service following Casey's wreck, it was ultimately scrapped.

Opposite: This is how the New York Central's famed 20th Century Limited looked in 1902 with six wooden cars trailing a Ten-Wheeler.

Right: Phoebe Snow was the fictional symbol of the Delaware, Lackawanna & Western which burned anthracite, so Phoebe's gown remained white.

Right: This all-steel car was built by American Car & Foundry for the New York Central in 1906. Early steel cars were quite heavy, but more sturdy in case of an accident.

Opposite top: Until the advent of heavyweight steel passenger cars, "Pacific"-type locomotives were adequate for most trains in the western US. The Great Northern assigned their Pacifics the "H" Class. H4 No.1445 was built by Baldwin in 1909.

Right: One of the most famous trains on the Southern Pacific was the Sunset Limited, which ran (and still runs under Amtrak) from Chicago to Los Angeles. The rich and famous enjoy the view from the observation car in 1910.

Opposite, bottom: It was a big event when the railroad came to town, bringing with it trains to seemingly everywhere. The first through train passes through Zanesville, Ohio, in 1909.

Below: The epitome of passenger power on the Pennsylvania Railroad was the K4 Pacific. Most of the 425 K4s were built by the PRR at its own shop in Altoona. They were assigned numbers scattered between 8 and 8378.

Bottom: A further refinement of the Pacific type led to the 4-6-4 "Hudson"-type. The extra axle on the trailing truck allowed for a bigger firebox. Wabash 706, built in 1925, was a semi-streamlined Hudson.

Opposite: Two of the Pennsylvania Railroad's K4 Pacifics were preserved. No.1361 was displayed at Horseshoe Curve until the mid-1980s, when it was removed and restored to excursion service.

Opposite: Consolidation-type No.40, built by Baldwin in 1925, originally powered freight trains for the Lancaster & Chester Railroad. It now hauls passenger cars full of tourists on the New Hope & Ivyland Railroad near Philadelphia, Pennsylvania.

Above: The Southern Railway's Ps-4 Pacifics were among the handsomest locomotives to operate. Painted in green and gold, the locomotives powered the Southern's premier trains southward from Washington, DC, and Cincinnati, Ohio.

Top: Equally handsome, and perhaps the ultimate in steam passenger power, were New York Central's J3a-Class Hudsons. Of the 275 Hudsons built for the NYC (50 of them Class J3a), none survived. The 5417 was built in 1926 by Lima.

The 4-8-4, or "Northern"-type, was a locomotive equally at home in freight and passenger service. Northern Pacific was the first railroad to acquire a 4-8-4, doing so in 1926 with a purchase of 12 from the American Locomotive Company. By 1941 the NP had acquired a total of 49 Northerns, with most coming from Baldwin. The Northern became the standard dual-service locomotive in North America, with practically every major railroad owning them. Many railroads eschewed the "Northern" moniker for the 4-8-4, however; alternate names included "Confederation" on the Canadian National and "Greenbrier" on the Chesapeake & Ohio.

SPECIFICATIONS

Wheel Arrange	4-8-4	Driving Wheels	73in (1,854mm)
Tractive Effort	69,800lb (31,660kg)	Builder	Baldwin
Weight	952,000lb (432t)	Length	105ft 4³/₈in (32,125mm)
		Year Built	1943

Northern Pacific No.2640 was in the A5 Class of Northerns, built by Baldwin in 1943, one of the final group of ten 4-8-4s purchased by the NP. The locomotive had a "centipede" tender, so named because of the multitude (actually 14) of wheels. The locomotives were assigned to a 999-mile run from St Paul, Minnesota, to Livingston, Montana. A nearly identical locomotive, Spokane, Portland & Seattle No.700, was restored to excursion service.

Left: The Chicago, Milwaukee, St Paul & Pacific (Milwaukee Road) had unique observation cars called Skytop Lounges. The windows extending up to the roof gave passengers a full panoramic view of the receding mountains as Milwaukee's trains crossed the western states.

Opposite: Two passenger trains sit in Los Angeles Union Passenger Terminal in a scene from about 1929. One of the trains is likely the Gold Coast Limited. LAUPT was often called "The Station of the Stars," as Hollywood's movie actors and actresses used the station frequently.

Below: Southern Pacific created its A-6 Class 4-4-2s by rebuilding Class A-3 locomotives that had been originally constructed in 1904-1906. No.3002 was rebuilt in 1925. The 4-4-2 "Atlantic"-types were speedsters, once you got them going. But with only four high driving wheels, they were quite slippery when starting a heavy train.

Left: A narrow gauge train traverses the Colorado mountains in the early 1930s on the Denver & Rio Grande (later the Denver & Rio Grande Western). On the point is a 2-8-2 locomotive.

Opposite: The Durango & Silverton Narrow Gauge Railroad carries passengers in much the same way as its predecessor, the Denver & Rio Grande, did in Colorado.

Below: The Overland Limited crosses the Lucin Cut-Off over the Great Salt Lake in Utah. Southern Pacific built the 30-mile-long causeway over the lake.

Right: A lounge car from the 1940s wasn't quite as ornate as those from the 1890s, but was comfortable nonetheless. Relaxing chairs, large windows, and fine food make the lounge the place to be on a train.

Opposite: The East Broad Top Railroad provided passenger service to the coal fields of south-central Pennsylvania until the 1930s. The EBT's narrow gauge is unusual for a railroad located in the eastern United States.

Right: The Santa Fe's food service was provided by the Fred Harvey Company. Not only did Harvey provide on-board meals, but it also established "Harvey Houses," with fine dining and lodging all along the route.

Right: Before Amtrak (and to some extent, even after Amtrak), dining was not the same on any two trains. Each railroad had its own china and silverware, and each had its own menus with specialty meals (such as Rocky Mountain Trout on the Rio Grande Zephyr). Cups, saucers, pitchers, plates, and coffee pots were unique to each railroad. Today, collecting railroad china remains one of the specialty hobbies within the entire rail enthusiast hobby.

Below: Ready for dinner—a table is elegantly set for the next meal. Dining on a train remains the highlight of any trip, even in the Amtrak age.

With the advent of the streamlined passenger trains and the diesel locomotive in the middle of the 20th Century, many railroads took to shrouding their steam power to give in a more "modern" look. Classic examples include the Southern Pacific's GS4 Northerns and the Norfolk & Western's J-Class Northerns and K-Class Mountains. The Milwaukee Road shrouded four Atlantics and six Hudsons for service on the railroad's Hiawathas. These trains attained speeds of 100mph.

Locomotive No.3 of the Chicago, Milwaukee, St Paul & Pacific (the Milwaukee Road) was one of four Atlantics streamlined by builder American Locomotive in 1935–37. The locomotives were capable of speeds of 100mph on the Hiawatha trains between Chicago, Illinois, and Minneapolis/St Paul, Minnesota.

SPECIFICATIONS

Wheel Arrange	4-4-2	Driving Wheels	84 in (2,134mm)
Tractive Effort	30,685lb (13,920kg)	Builder	American Locomotive
Weight	537,000lb (244t)	Length	88ft 8in (27,026mm)
		Year Built	1935

Right: The Boston & Albany used 4-6-4T (the "T" stood for "tank," which meant the locomotive had no tender) locomotives in the Boston area.

Below: The Baltimore & Ohio's Pacifics were called the "President" Class by the railroad. No.3500, the President Washington, is preserved.

Right: One of Canadian Pacific's mammoth 2-10-4s, No.5000, sits in Windsor Station in Montreal. Note the bell mounted low on the pilot. Windsor Station ultimately became a commuter-only facility, with inter-city trains using Central Station.

Above: The New York, New Haven & Hartford Railroad streamlined its Hudsons for service between New Haven, Connecticut, and Boston, Massachusetts. Note the "disk" driving wheels.

Opposite: Railroads promoted their passenger services in a variety of colorful ways. Posters attracted people to the trains, and bright timetables told the scenic virtues of each line (in addition to listing the schedules). Once on the train, the promotion didn't stop. You could play games in the lounge with a deck of playing cards that had the logo of the train or railroad. You could get an ornament for your desk, or even a pair of scissors or a letter opener.

Left: Santa Fe's only streamlined steam locomotive was Hudson No. 3460, called the Blue Goose. The locomotive was built by Baldwin in 1937 for passenger service between Chicago, Illinois, and La Junta, Colorado.

Left: On the 50th anniversary of transcontinental service on the Canadian Pacific Railway, a properly adorned train is ready to depart from Montreal's Windsor Station on June 28, 1936.

Below: A 4-8-4 is ready to assist a heavy passenger train over the mountains in western Canada on the Canadian Pacific. While most railroads called their 4-8-4s "Northerns," on the CPR they were known as "Selkirks," in honor of one of the mountain ranges the line crosses in British Columbia.

Opposite: The premier train for the Chicago & North Western was the "400," departing Chicago in 1939. The train was re-equipped by 1940 with streamlined equipment.

Opposite: Union Pacific train, The 49er, is on its first run at Evansville, Wyoming, in 1939. This train operated five times a month between Chicago and the Golden Gate Exposition in San Francisco. The 49er ran until 1941.

Below: Union Pacific shrouded two locomotives in streamlined casings in 1937, one of which was 4-8-2 No. 7002 (along with Pacific No. 2906). These two locomotives provided emergency protection service for the diesel-equipped "City" streamliners operated by the railroad. The two locomotives were eventually assigned to The 49er.

While many 4-8-4s were dual-service (passenger and freight), the Northerns of the Chicago, Burlington & Quincy were relegated to primarily freight service. One of the O5A Class, however, would ultimately achieve fame hauling passengers. The reason the O5s spent most of their career in freight service was because the CB&Q (or the Burlington Route) was a pioneer in using streamlined diesel power from General Motors, plus the railroad had a fine fleet of 4-6-4 Hudsons.

SPECIFICATIONS

Wheel Arrange	4-8-4
Tractive Effort	67,500lb (30,626kg)
Weight	838,050lb (380.2t)
Driving Wheels	74in (1,879mm)
Builder	Burlington
Length	105ft 11in (32,283mm)
Year Built	1939

Burlington Route No.5626 was one of 15 modern O5s (classified as O5A) the railroad built in its own shops. Sister locomotive 5632 went on to fame heading up the Burlington's steam program in the early 1960s when excursions were held for railroad enthusiasts. Five of the big Northerns were donated to towns along the Burlington when steam operations ended.

Left: The Canadian Pacific was (and is) one of North America's most scenic railroads, especially in the West. A passenger train traverses the Frasier River Canyon in the 1930s near Yale, British Columbia. The railroad also traversed the Thompson River Canyon.

Above: High-stepping Erie Railroad No.2960 leads the New York-Chicago Express away from the Hudson River for its journey westward. The Erie, like most eastern railroads, served New York City via ferry from New Jersey.

Left: The Louisville & Nashville Railroad served the cities between Cincinnati, Ohio, and New Orleans, Louisiana. Its premier train, the Pan American, was heard live every day but Sunday as it passed the studios of WSM radio (home of the Grand Ole Opry) during the 1930s and 1940s. Other L&N trains included the South Wind and the Dixie Flagler.

Left: Under the grandeur of the western Canada mountains, a Canadian Pacific train runs over the railroad's transcontinental main line in the province of Alberta.

Right: A typical passenger car in the pre-streamlined era looked pretty much like this. Utilitarian, yet comfortable, this was the way to travel quickly from town to town. Even these spartan accommodations are more comfortable than today's modern airliners.

Right: The railroads proved their worth during times of war, especially both World Wars. During the First World War the US railroads were nationalized, but during World War II they remained independent, although there were restrictions placed on them by the government.

Below: The Baltimore & Ohio's premier train, the Royal Blue, crosses Thomas Viaduct at Relay, Maryland, in 1940. At the time the bridge was 105 years old and is still in service as the 21st Century begins.

Above: Coaches through the years include (left to right, bottom to top): carriages from 1831; a typical coach from 1856; a clerestory roof coach from 1868; a semi-vestibule coach from 1894; a 1907 all steel coach, and a stainless steel coach from 1939.

Left: Southern Pacific painted entire passenger trains, including the locomotive, in the attractive "Daylight" paint scheme.

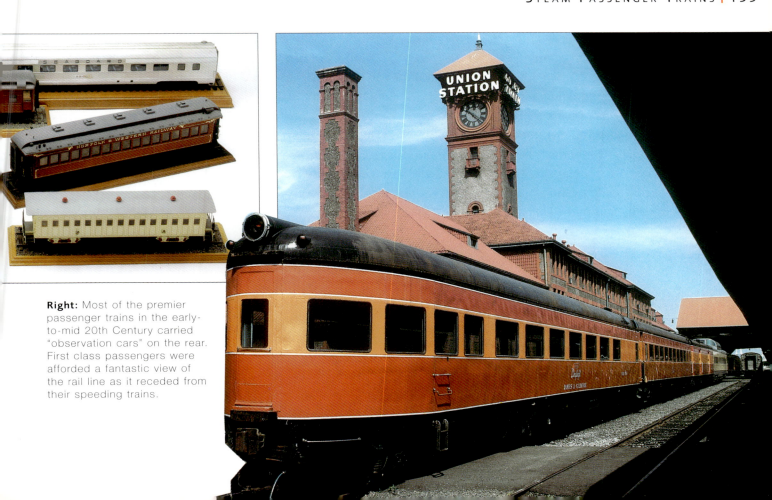

Right: Most of the premier passenger trains in the early-to-mid 20th Century carried "observation cars" on the rear. First class passengers were afforded a fantastic view of the rail line as it receded from their speeding trains.

The New York Central's passenger line from New York to Chicago, dubbed the "Water Level Route" as it followed the Hudson River and the Great Lakes, was moving record numbers of people as the Second World War was ending. Passenger trains were getting larger than what the classic Hudsons could handle, so the NYC invested in several 4-8-4s. While most railroads called their 4-8-4s "Northerns," the NYC called them "Niagaras" and assigned Class S1 to them. In all, 27 were built. Some steam experts have claimed the Niagara to be the ultimate locomotive, a claim that would surely be challenged by fans of the Union Pacific or Norfolk & Western.

New York Central's Niagaras measured over 115ft from coupler to coupler but could fit on a 100ft turntable, thanks to the last wheels on the tender being tucked in from the rear. Despite being the pinnacle of steam, no Niagaras nor their famous NYC cousins, the J3 Hudsons, were preserved.

SPECIFICATIONS

Wheel Arrange	4-8-4
Tractive Effort	61,570lb (27,936kg)
Weight	274,000lb (124t)
Driving Wheels	79in (2,006mm)
Builder	American Locomotive
Length	115ft 5½in (35,192mm)
Year Built	1945

Below: Throughout the 20th Century, there were exhibitions that touted the latest developments in railroad technology and entertained the public. Among the most famous was the "Fair of the Iron Horse" held by the Baltimore & Ohio in 1927 and "Railroads on Parade" as a part of the 1939–40 World's Fair in New York. The California State Railroad Museum has held three Railfairs as recently as 1981, 1991, and 1999, and restored steam locomotives were a big part of Expo86, the World's Fair in Vancouver, British Columbia.

Above: Passenger railroad advertising posters were works of art, showing the public what scenic thrills they could experience while on the train. The Southern Pacific and the San Diego & Arizona both touted the appeal of train travel through California.

Opposite: One of Southern Pacific's Class GS4 4-8-4 locomotives was returned to service in the 1980s for excursion service. It was united with many passenger cars from the SP's Daylight service, creating one of the most striking excursion trains in the United States.

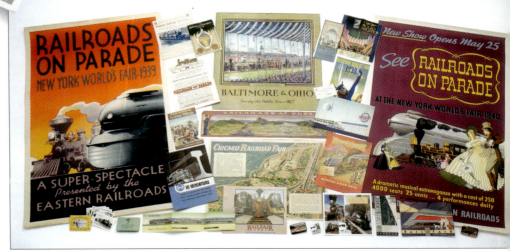

Below: Southern Pacific boasted some of the handsomest locomotives operating in passenger service anywhere in North America. Trim "Pacifics" such as No.2472 hauled light trains, while large "Northerns" such as No.4449 in Daylight colors powered longer, heavier trains. Diesels supplanted steam on SP passenger trains in the 1950s.

Above: Two generations of Golden State passenger power met at Railfair 1999, held at the California State Railroad Museum in Sacramento. Southern Pacific No.2467 was built by Baldwin in 1921 and remained in service until the late 1950s. Amtrak No.456 was built by the Electro-Motive Division of General Motors in 1998 for service throughout California.

Right: Steam locos still haul passenger trains throughout the US, although only in tourist service. The Strasburg Rail Road in Pennsylvania is the most successful tourist railroad, carrying nearly a half million riders each year. Over 100 steam locomotives operate each year.

4

Stations

As railroads became the arteries that supplied the economic blood to the growing countries of the United States and Canada, stations were soon appearing in every town. Entire books could be devoted to railroad architecture, but a distinct style emerged that said, "This building is a railroad station," no matter if it was on the Pennsylvania Railroad or the Delaware, Lackawanna & Western. Meanwhile, big city stations were being built to grand scales, only rivalled by the churches in architectural magnificence. The railroad station became one of the social centers in any town, as anyone who was leaving or coming into the community came through the station.

Left: Los Angeles Union Passenger Terminal was the gateway to Hollywood, used by movie stars in the 1940s and 1950s.

Right: One of the greatest stations ever built was Pennsylvania Station in New York City. Used by the Pennsylvania Railroad as well as the Long Island Rail Road and the New York, New Haven & Hartford, the magnificent structure was demolished in 1964, replaced by a new station with no character in the basement of Madison Square Garden.

Opposite: Small-town depots, such as the one at West Cressona, Pennsylvania, were often the center of social life as the townsfolks would come down to the tracks to see the daily passenger train.

Below: A freight train approaches a wood frame station on the former Delaware, Lackawanna & Western main line at Cresco, Pennsylvania. The dark green color is typical of most of the Lackawanna's stations. The train works for DL&W successor Delaware-Lackawanna Railway.

Above: Most stations had a baggage room where passengers could check baggage through to their destination, much like airlines do today. Amtrak still accepts checked baggage, but only at larger towns and cities.

Opposite: Just after sunrise, passengers prepare to board an Amtrak express train bound for New York City at the station at Wilmington, Delaware. This station was built by the Pennsylvania Railroad.

Right: The East Strasburg, Pennsylvania, station is brightly decorated for the Christmas season. The station serves the five-mile-long Strasburg Rail Road.

Profile: Lancaster Station

The Pennsylvania Railroad, which proclaimed itself the "Standard Railroad of the World," always did things in a grand way. In the 1930s it electrified its main line between New York and Washington to provide high-speed passenger service. At the same time, it electrified its line through eastern Pennsylvania between Philadelphia and the state capital at Harrisburg. From Philadelphia's 30th Street Station westward to Paoli the tracks ran through some of the wealthiest sections of Philadelphia (and these areas are still known as the "Main Line" in honor of the PRR), but beyond Paoli the tracks entered farmlands which were (and are) home to the Amish farmers.

The largest city between Philadelphia and Harrisburg is Lancaster, deep in Pennsylvania's Amish country. Lancaster's station is a bit large for the size of the city, but as the center for economic commerce in Lancaster County, the PRR obviously deemed the city worthy of a fine station. Like many PRR stations, including Philadelphia and Harrisburg, the Lancaster station fell into disarray in the 1960s but was restored to its glory in the 1990s.

Right: As part of the celebration for the 60th Anniversary of the National Railway Historical Society in 1995, vintage cars were brought to the former Pennsylvania Railroad (now Amtrak) station in Lancaster, Pennsylvania, to create a scene from the first half of the 20th Century.

PENNSYLVANIA RAILROAD

Left: Buffalo's Central Station was built by the New York Central just as passenger trains were beginning to decline in the 1930s. Located away from the downtown area, the grand station never lived up to its full potential and was closed when Amtrak took over passenger service in 1971.

Below, right: Monroe, North Carolina, was a junction point on Seaboard Air Line. The SAL's line from Hamlet, North Carolina, split at Monroe, with one line going into Charlotte, North Carolina, and another heading to Atlanta, Georgia.

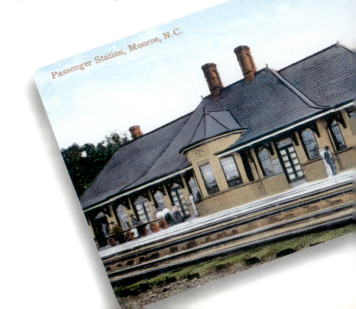

Wilmington, Brunswick & Southern Railroad—Train leaving Station, Southport, N.C.

Left: The Wilmington, Brunswick & Southern operated in North Carolina from the Atlantic Ocean coastal town of Southport to a connection with the Seaboard Air Line at Wilmington.

Below: Several railroads were funnelled through Montgomery, Alabama, at the city's Union Station including: the Louisville & Nashville; Seaboard Air Line; Atlantic Coast Line; Western Railway of Alabama; and Mobile & Ohio.

MONTGOMERY, ALA.
Union Passenger Station.

Terminal Station and Union Depot, Mobile, Ala.

Opposite: The eastern end of the Texas & Pacific was located in New Orleans, Louisiana. From here, the railroad crossed the entire state of Texas before terminating in El Paso.

Below: At Paris, Kentucky, the Louisville & Nashville's branch line from the Ohio River at Maysville, Kentucky, joined the road's main line from Cincinnati, Ohio. This branch later became the Trans Kentucky Railroad and hosted a tourist railroad for several years.

L. & N. R. R. Station, Paris, Ky.

Above: The Mobile & Ohio served its southern terminal of Mobile, Alabama, with a magnificent Union Station. Today the tracks are gone but the structure survives.

Texas and Pacific Passenger Station, New Orleans, La.

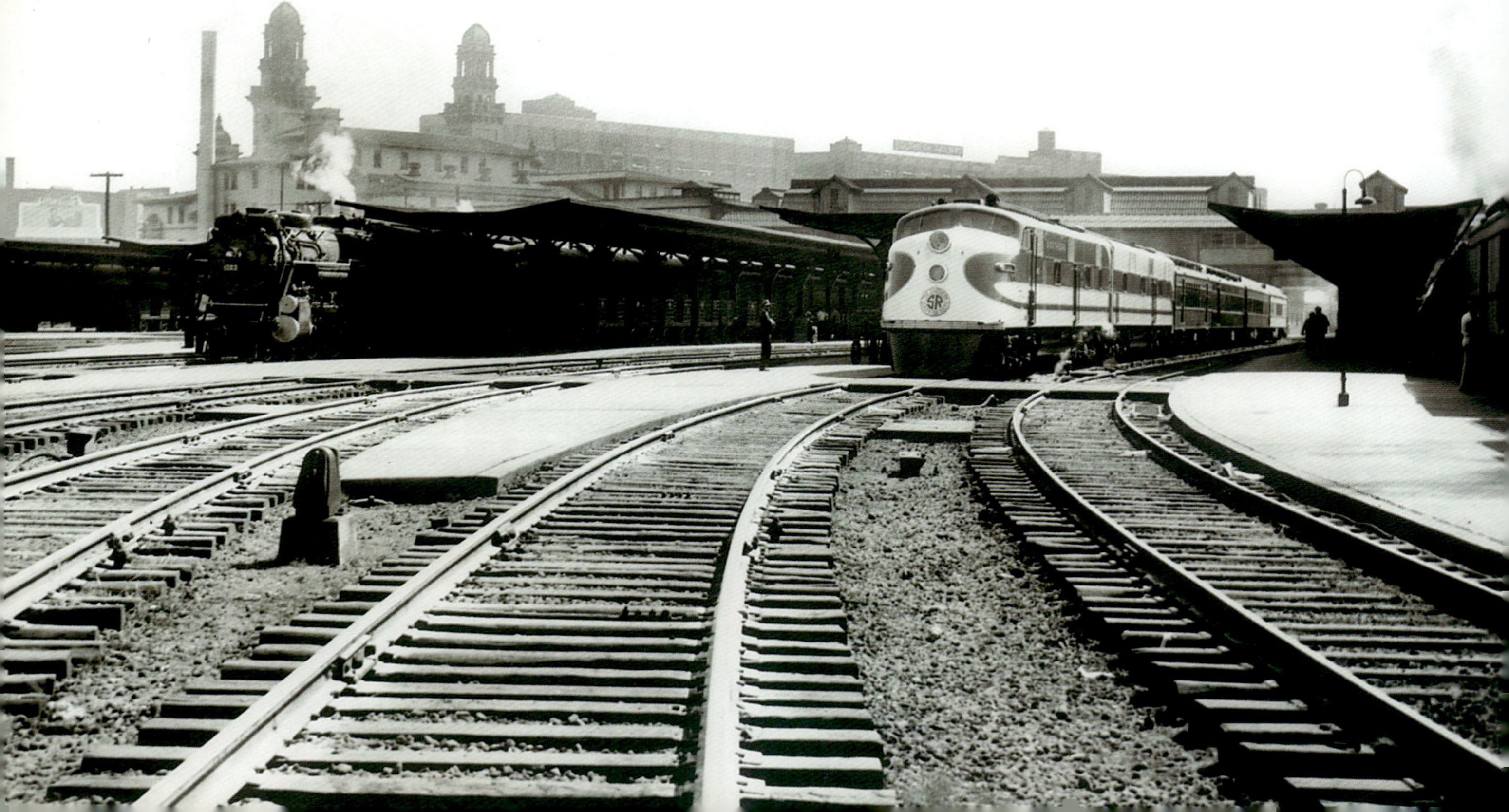
SR

Opposite: In the mid-1940s, the Crescent of the Southern Railway pauses in Atlanta, Georgia, behind a pair of E6 passenger locomotives. Train No.40, an Atlanta-to-Washington train with no name, is also in the station behind a 4-6-2 steam locomotive.

Right: This typical wood frame depot was located on the Grand Trunk Railway at St Williams, Ontario. This station was built in the late 19th Century. The Grand Trunk is a subsidiary of the Canadian National Railway.

Profile: Union Station, Nashville

Officially opened on October 9, 1900, Nashville Union Station boasted one of the largest single-span gable-roof trainsheds in the United States, stretching out beyond a Romanesque headhouse. Many cities had "union" stations—stations used by more than one railroad—which made connections easier for passengers. Nashville Union Station had two railroads—the Louisville & Nashville, and the Nashville, Chattanooga & St Louis (which by the time the station opened was a subsidiary of the L&N).

For over half a decade, the L&N's most famous trains, including the Dixie Limited and the Southwind, stopped at the station. By the time Amtrak took over passenger train operations in the United States on May 1, 1971, Union Station had fallen on hard times, and Amtrak's lone Chicago-to-Florida train did not use the facility due to its size. In fact, by 1980 Amtrak no longer served Nashville at all. Nonetheless, the impressive magnificence of the building eventually led to its being restored as one of Nashville's finest hotels, one of the earliest conversions of its type (in later years, other large stations, including those in St Louis, Missouri, and Scranton, Pennsylvania, would be converted to hotels). While the hotel assured the salvation of the headhouse, the trainshed remained vacant. Despite its inclusion in the National Historic Landmarks program, the shed was ultimately torn down.

The station's large clock tower is famous for never being accurate—even today it keeps time poorly.

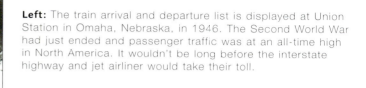

Left: The train arrival and departure list is displayed at Union Station in Omaha, Nebraska, in 1946. The Second World War had just ended and passenger traffic was at an all-time high in North America. It wouldn't be long before the interstate highway and jet airliner would take their toll.

Below: The Missouri Pacific's station at Kirkwood, Missouri, is still a place where people gather to watch trains. A comfortable park across the tracks (now owned by the Union Pacific), provides a pleasant place for a summer cook-out.

Opposite: The Capitol Limited of the Baltimore & Ohio and Train No. 8 of the Chesapeake & Ohio are ready to depart from Chicago. Train sheds spanning many tracks were common in large cities, but none remain in service today.

Right: The Yellowstone Special pauses at the station in Salt Lake City, Utah, in 1910. The locomotive is being serviced and the baggage loaded in anticipation of the train's departure. The UP's Salt Lake City station, as well as the neighboring Denver & Rio Grande station still survive, and UP still uses its station for offices.

Opposite: Union Pacific's station in Salt Lake City, Utah, proudly bears the railroad's herald in neon lights. Passenger trains no longer call at this station, using the nearby Rio Grande station instead.

Left: Amtrak's California Zephyr pauses at the station in Salt Lake City, Utah. The station was originally constructed by the Denver & Rio Grande Western.

Right: The Union Station in Denver, Colorado, sits in an area of the city that is being revitalized. Once used by the Union Pacific, the Denver & Rio Grande Western and the Chicago, Burlington & Quincy, today only Amtrak's California Zephyr stops on its way between Chicago and San Francisco. Coors Field, home of baseball's Colorado Rockies, was built just a few blocks from the station in the early 1990s.

Below: As passenger services declined in the United States and Canada, new stations were seldom needed. When a new station was built, it was often quite spartan, such as the VIA Rail Canada facility in Saskatoon, Saskatchewan.

Above: The Union Pacific's station in Salt Lake City is still a busy place, although only freight trains rumble by. The last passenger service was taken from the station at the formation of Amtrak in 1971. Nonetheless, the junction next to the station is seldom quiet, as many transcontinental freights make their way through the Utah city.

Profile: Denver Union Station

As the railroads built westward, they tried to circumnavigate the Rocky Mountains by various means. The Union Pacific crossed the Continental Divide on Sherman Hill in Wyoming, where the hills are less rugged. The Atchison, Topeka & Santa Fe, and the Southern Pacific headed south to bypass the most rugged portion of the Rockies. Even the Denver & Rio Grande Western, when looking to head west from Denver, decided to build southward to Pueblo before heading west and attacking the Rockies through the Royal Gorge and over Tennessee Pass. But with the completion of the Moffat Tunnel in 1928, at long last a railroad attacked the heart of the Rockies. Soon the Rio Grande's passenger business was flourishing as folks rode the "Scenic Route of the West."

Denver Union Station was the eastern terminal for the D&RGW, and the station was also served by the Chicago, Burlington & Quincy from the east, as well as the Fort Worth & Denver, a Union Pacific branch from Cheyenne, and a Santa Fe branch. When Amtrak was formed in 1971, the Rio Grande was one of three railroads that opted to keep running its own passenger trains (along with the Rock Island and the Southern). Ultimately, the Rio Grande operated the last non-Amtrak intercity train in the United States—the Rio Grande Zephyr between Denver and Salt Lake City, Utah. Denver Union Station served as the gateway for riders coming to ride America's last streamliner. Despite falling on hard times, the station and its surrounding area is being revitalized.

For the first time since the blackouts imposed by World War II, Denver Union Station was illuminated for Christmas in 1999. The station is in Denver's Lower Downtown area (LoDo), which is being revitalized as a night life area, with fine pubs and restaurants. The baseball stadium for the Colorado Rockies, Coors Field, is located just three blocks from the station. Amtrak's California Zephyr still stops daily.

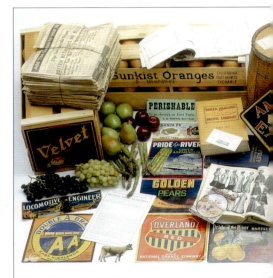

Below: Express shipments were once big business on the railroads. Railway Express Agency had cars in passenger trains to expedite the movement of perishables, and many passenger trains in rural areas carried cans of milk direct from the dairy farm to the big city. Amtrak has continued the duties of Railway Express Agency, moving express freight on its passenger trains.

Above: Amtrak's California Zephyr makes a stop at Union Station in Denver, Colorado, on its eastward journey from San Francisco to Chicago. The train has just descended the spectacular Front Range of the Rocky Mountains.

Right: Glacier National Park, located near the Canadian border in Montana, is served by a station located just outside the park. Built by the Great Northern, the line ultimately became a part of the Burlington Northern & Santa Fe system, while Amtrak provides passenger service. Many of the National Parks in the west were developed by railroads as a destination for passengers.

Right: The magnificent station at Whitefish, Montana, was constructed by the Great Northern. A large station for a small town, its size can be attributed to the fact that Whitefish is a division point (railroad divisions extend 100 miles). Many small towns that were division points had large depots to house the many divisional offices that needed to be located at each point.

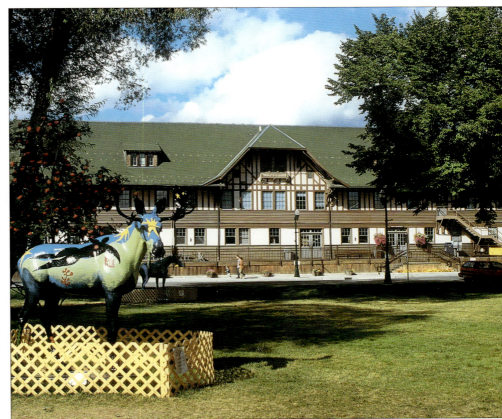

Left: The ticket office for Canadian National in Prince Rupert, British Columbia, was a storefront. The wooden sidewalk and dirt road indicate that Prince Rupert is on the edge of civilization in this 1920s view. Even in the early 21st Century, Prince Rupert is still on the edge of civilization in the northern reaches of western Canada.

Below: Edmonds, Washington, sported a "modern" station in the 1950s. Edmonds is located on the Great Northern (later Burlington Northern and today Burlington Northern & Santa Fe), outside Seattle. In this scene, the station, the automobiles, and the passenger diesels are all brand new.

Opposite: A turn-of-the-century train arrives at Union Pacific's depot at Hood River, Oregon. UP cut across the northern side of Oregon through the Columbia River Gorge on its way to Portland. On the opposite side of the Gorge, in the state of Washington, was the Spokane, Portland & Seattle (now a part of Burlington Northern & Santa Fe).

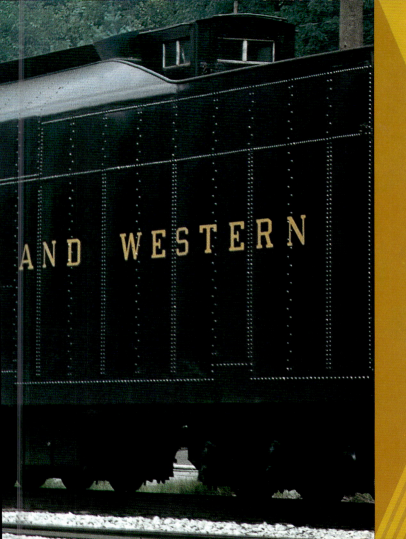

5

Super Steam Trains

Some steam locomotives were "super" when built—extraordinary in size, speed, or power. Others became "super" in later years by virtue of being restored in the diesel era. These locomotives became famous as survivors and found favor among thousands of railroad enthusiasts. Super steam, indeed!

Left: Norfolk & Western Class A No.1218 pulls into Iaeger, West Virginia, with an excursion in July 1991.

Right: One of the Chesapeake & Ohio Allegheny No.1622 rolls off the turntable at Huntington, West Virginia. The 2-6-6-6 Alleghenies, along with Norfolk & Western's A-Class 2-6-6-4s, were the biggest and best steam to operate in the eastern United States.

Opposite: New York Central's Hudsons were among the finest passenger steam power ever developed. Designer Henry Dreyfuss added the streamlining to the 20th Century Limited and its locomotive.

Left: Southern Pacific's AC-Class 4-8-8-2s were of the "Cab Forward" design. This kept the crew ahead of the locomotive's smoke in the railroad's long tunnels in the Sierra Nevada mountains on the California-Nevada border.

Opposite: The Chesapeake & Ohio's George Washington pauses at the station at White Sulpher Springs, West Virginia, behind a Pacific that has a workhorse look to it, thanks to the air pumps hanging from the smokebox.

Above: Canadian Pacific semi-streamlined 45 of its 4-6-4s, creating the railroad's "Royal Hudsons." Two of these fine locomotives operated in tourist service, No.2839 for the Southern Railway in the US, and No.2860 for BC Rail in Canada.

Below: Union Pacific FEF-3 No.844 operated for less than 20 years in regular service, but has been in excursion for over 40 years. It was renumbered 8444 when first placed in excursion service, but was ultimately given its original number back in 1990.

Above: Union Pacific 4-8-4 No.844 was built by the American Locomotive Company in 1944. It was assigned No.8444 in 1960 when a GP30 diesel was given No.844. The big Northern operated as No.8444 for 30 years.

Left: In the Colorado desert, Union Pacific 8444 performs a "photo runby" during an excursion from Denver to Sterling. Passengers are unloaded from the train, then the train backs up and races past the passengers for the benefit of their cameras.

Left: The Pennsylvania Railroad's T1 Class 4-4-4-4s may have been the most famous streamlined steam locomotive in America. With streamlining designed by Raymond Loewy, the T1s were built for hauling passenger trains quickly across the flatlands of Ohio and Indiana. Alas, even on level ground, the tall drivers gave little adhesion when starting, and ultimately all of the T1s were scrapped.

The Lima Locomotive Works of Lima, Ohio, came about as close as any builder to perfecting the steam locomotive. With its Berkshires for the Nickel Plate and Northerns for the Southern Pacific, Lima "Super Power" was still moving trains long after diesels had made major inroads into most railroad's motive power. The SP had 60 Northerns built by Lima (along with 14 from Baldwin), decked out in one of the most classic paint schemes ever applied to a steam locomotive—the black, maroon, and orange of the Daylight trains.

SPECIFICATIONS

Wheel Arrange	4-8-4	Driving Wheels	80in (2,032mm)
Tractive Effort	71,173lb (32,285kg)	Builder	Lima
Weight	883,000lb (400.5t)	Gauge	4ft 8.5in (1435mm)
		Year Built	1941

The GS-2 Class of SP 4-8-4s, such as No.4412, were slightly smaller than the later GS-3, GS-4, GS-5, and GS-6 Classes. GS-4 No.4449 powered the American Freedom Train in 1975–76, decked out in red, white, and blue.

Opposite: Union Pacific Big Boy No.4007 rides the turntable at Ogden, Utah, in 1942. Originally assigned to freights in the Wahsatch Mountains of Utah, the Big Boys would finish their careers on Sherman Hill in Wyoming.

Above: Yellowstone No.222 of the Duluth, Missabe & Iron Range poses for a portrait in 1941. The 2-8-8-4s were assigned Class M3 by the DM&IR.

Top: The "Yellowstones" of the Duluth, Missabe & Iron Range were built to haul ore in Minnesota. The massive locomotives, built by Baldwin, could haul 190 loaded ore cars. The Northern Pacific was the first railroad to use locomotives of the 2-8-8-4 arrangement.

Below: Two former Norfolk & Western steam locomotives charge side by side up Christiansburg Mountain in 1987, 30 years after the N&W dieselized.

Above: Norfolk & Western's 4-8-4s had smaller drivers than most Northerns, due to the mountains on the railroad, but still achieved speeds of 90mph.

Right: Spokane, Portland & Seattle 4-8-4 No.700 returned to its home rails in 2001 in excursion service. The big Northern type was built by the Baldwin Locomotive Works in 1938.

Below: Norfolk & Western 2-6-6-4 No.1218 is right at home in the yard at Iaeger, West Virginia, in 1991. No.1218 worked this line in regular service in the 1950s.

Right: Atlanta & West Point 4-6-2 No.290 was built by the Lima Locomotive Works in 1926. It later served on the New Georgia Railroad near Atlanta.

Below: Saint Louis-San Francisco (The "Frisco") had a fleet of 63 Mountain-type 4-8-2 locomotives for both freight and passenger service. No.1522 was preserved at the National Museum of Transportation in St Louis, and restored to operation.

Above: The St Louis Southwestern Railway was more commonly called the Cotton Belt. Northern-type No.819 is maintained at the railroad's former shop complex (converted to a museum), and became the last Cotton Belt steam locomotive to operate.

While Union Pacific's 4-8-8-4 "Big Boys" got most of the glory, being the largest steam locomotives to ever operate in North America, the railroad's slightly smaller 4-6-6-4 were equally workhorses. But while the small-drivered Big Boys were working freight, the high-stepping Challengers were at home on the front of passenger trains. The first UP Challenger was delivered in 1936, with the final order placed in 1944 during the Second World War. They remained in service until 1956, when dieselization finally caught up with the biggest passenger steam power in the world.

SPECIFICATIONS

Wheel Arrange	4-6-6-4	Driving Wheels	69in (1,753mm)
Tractive Effort	97,400lb (44,100kg)	Builder	American Locomotive
Weight	1,071,000lb (486t)	Length	121ft 11in (37,160mm)
		Year Built	1942

Challenger No.3977 wears the two-tone gray paint applied to UP's passenger steam power. Sister locomotive No.3985 was restored to service in the 1980s, becoming the largest operating steam locomotive in the world as the 21st Century began.

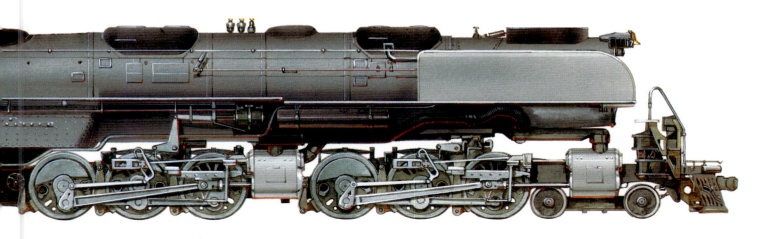

Below: With the success of Northern 844 in excursion service, Union Pacific restored Challenger-type No.3985 to operation. No.3985 became the largest steam locomotive to operate in the post-steam era.

Above: Cotton Belt No.819 works on its old home line in Arkansas as it heads for St Louis, Missouri, in 1990.

Opposite: No.819 crosses the Mississippi River at Thebes, Missouri, during a 1990 trip to St Louis. The locomotive was restored by volunteer workers of the Cotton Belt Historical Society in Pine Bluff, Arkansas.

Below: A Union Pacific freight is ready to tackle the grade of Sherman Hill as it passes the tower at Borie, Wyoming. A pair of the railroad's articulated locomotives lead the train on its climb over the Continental Divide.

Right: The UP expansion of the 1980s and 1990s resulted in its excursion locomotives operating over trackage they had never been on before. Challenger No.3985 soared over Clio Viaduct on the former Western Pacific, California in 1992.

Below: Sherman Hill, located just west of Cheyenne, Wyoming, was perhaps the most famous location on the Union Pacific in the days of steam. In the excursion era, Challenger No.3985 returns to familiar rails on Sherman for a 1986 excursion sponsored by the Rocky Mountain Railroad Club of Denver, Colorado.

Right: The Union Pacific wasn't the only railroad to operate Challenger-type locomotives. Among the other roads to own Challengers was the Clinchfield, which operated in the mountains of Kentucky and Tennessee. All of the original Clinchfield Challengers were scrapped when the line dieselized, however. In 1992, CSX (successor railroad to the Clinchfield) borrowed Union Pacific No.3985 and disguised it as "Clinchfield No.676."

Opposite: The steam preservation movement has resulted in the recreation of scenes no one could have envisioned would ever happen again. After the Clinchfield scrapped all its Challengers, who could have possibly believed that a 4-6-6-4 would ever return to Kingsport, Tennessee. But when the Santa Claus Specials (originally operated by the Clinchfield), celebrated their 50th Anniversary in 1992, CSX and Union Pacific teamed up to return a Clinchfield Challenger to the Appalachian Mountains.

Above: Santa Fe had 65 4-8-4s on its roster, all built by Baldwin. No.3751 was ultimately restored to excursion service in 1991.

Below: Canadian National 4-8-2 No.6060 prepares to depart Union Station in Toronto, Ontario, with an excursion in 1980.

Opposite: The San Bernardino Railroad Historical Society's former Santa Fe 4-8-4 No.3751 is on home rails in the Tehachapi Mountains in California in 1999.

The Canadian National Railway purchased a total of 79 4-8-2 "Mountain"-type locomotives, starting with 16 from the Canadian Locomotive Company in 1923. Used in Montreal-to-Toronto passenger service, the locomotives attained speeds in excess of 80mph. The final 20 locomotives, purchased from the Montreal Locomotive Works in 1944 and painted an attractive green, were given the name "Bullet Nosed Bettys," due to the cone applied to the front of the smokebox.

Canadian National 4-8-2 No.6060 survived dieselization and was restored to service in the late 1970s, when it powered Toronto-to-Niagara Falls excursions. These trips often exceeded 80mph, showing that this Bullet Nosed Betty could still strut her stuff.

SPECIFICATIONS

Wheel Arrange	4-8-2	Driving Wheels	73in (1,854mm)
Tractive Effort	52,500lb (23,814kg)	Builder	Montreal
Weight	638,000lb (290t)	Length	93ft 3in (28,426mm)
		Year Built	1944

Right: The most famous locomotives built by Lima Locomotive Works of Ohio were arguably the 2-8-4 Berkshire-types purchased by several railroads. Two survivors, one each from the Nickel Plate and Pere Marquette, run together in 1991.

Below: Nickel Plate No.765 was built by Lima in 1944. It rests at Meadow Creek, West Virginia, while powering the famous New River Train, an annual excursion from Huntington, West Virginia.

Above: Pere Marquette No.1225 is another of the famous Lima-built Berkshires, coming out of the builder's erecting shop in 1941. No.1225 was on display in Michigan before being returned to excursion service.

Right: Restored to service in the same shop it was built in some 40 years before, Reading Company 4-8-4 No.2102 is prepared for service at Reading, Pennsylvania, in 1984. The Reading had 28 of the big Northerns.

Opposite: Canadian Pacific 4-8-4 No.5920 leads The Dominion through the Rocky Mountains in 1948. The CPR called their 4-8-4s "Selkirks," while most other railroads called them "Northerns."

Above: With the fuel crisis of the 1970s, a proposal was put forth to build a new, modern coal-fired steam locomotive. Just as quickly, the energy crisis ended and the plans for the ACE 3000 vanished along with it.

Below: Once the diesel locomotive was the undisputed future of railroad power, steam locomotives were retired at an incredible rate during the 1950s. Long lines of locomotives awaiting scrapping were common all across the US.

6

Diesel Freight Trains

The diesel locomotive first made its mark in hauling freight. Unlike steam locomotives, which required a full crew for every locomotive on the train, multiple diesels could be operated by one crew from the lead unit. Less labor intensive than steam, it didn't take long for the new locomotives to appear in great numbers.

Left: An FA1 and RS3, both manufactured by the American Locomotive Company, pull a train of vintage cars in 1986.

Left: Diesels produced by the American Locomotive Company were collectively known as "Alcos." A T6 works on the Middletown & Hummelstown. The T6 model was introduced in 1958.

Below: Introduced in 1940, Alco's "S" series came in variations from the S1 (1940) through the S13 (1959). The Stockton Terminal & Eastern operated S1s, S2s, and S4s on its switching railroad in California.

Right: The most popular Alco roadswitchers were the "RS" (Road Switcher) series. While the RS1 and RS2 models sold over 400 units each, the RS3 accumulated over 1,200 sales.

Above: Alco's big road units were of the "Century" series, which had a "C" as a prefix letter. Reading Company No.5308, a C630, leads a coal train on the Reading & Northern in the Pennsylvania coal fields.

Opposite: Unique to Canada were RS18 locomotives, built by the Montreal Locomotive Works based on designs by Alco. Canadian Pacific owned the bulk of the RS18s. Many went to short lines after retirement by CPR.

Right: A Canadian National M420 works in Halifax, Nova Scotia. The M420s, built by the Montreal Locomotive Works, were identical to the C420s built by Alco in the United States. Most Alco Century models had a Canadian-built equivalent.

Following the success of a demonstration locomotive in 1924 that showed diesel locomotives were viable in the railroad environment, General Electric and Ingersoll-Rand teamed up to build 26 boxy locomotives between 1924 and 1926. While 14 went to industrial customers, 12 were purchased by main line railroads including the: Baltimore & Ohio; Central Railroad of New Jersey; Chicago & North Western; Erie; Reading; Delaware, Lackawanna & Western and Lehigh Valley. Most of the railroads bought them for use in the New York City area, where steam locomotive smoke was beginning to cause a great deal of pollution. While it would be another 20 years before diesels began to make major inroads into the ranks of steam, these pioneers were the first to put the writing on the wall.

SPECIFICATIONS	
Builder	American Locomotive
Tractive Effort	
Weight	120,000lb (54.4t)
Wheel Arrange	B-B
Length	32ft 6in (9,906mm)
Max. Axleload	30,000lb (13.6t)
Year Built	1924

Central Railroad of New Jersey No. 1000 was one of the first commercially successful diesel locomotives. Built in 1924, it served into the 1950s before being preserved at the Museum of Transportation near St Louis, Missouri.

Left: Reading Company C630 No.5308 poses with GP30 No.5513 outside the railroad's main shop in Reading, Pennsylvania. The 5308 was built by Alco in 1967, while the 5513 was built by EMD in 1962.

Above: The Cape Breton & Central Nova Scotia was one of the last railroads to operate a large fleet of "Big Alcos." The line operated M630s (the Montreal Locomotive Works' version of Alco's C630), into the late 1990s.

Below: The Electro-Motive Division of General Motors began producing the extremely popular "F" series in 1939 when the FT was introduced. Following an interim "F2" model, the F3 was put into production in 1945, with 1,111 "A" units and 696 "B" units constructed. An "A-B" set of F3s were restored and painted for the Jersey Central in 1991.

Below: One of the last freight assignments on a major railroad for F-units was the Nanticoke Steel Train on Canadian National. An A-B-A set of F7s was assigned to the train in the late 1980s.

Above: An FPA4 built by the Montreal Locomotive Works for Canadian National in 1959 meets an F7 built by EMD for the Wabash in 1953. The scene is at the Monticello Railway Museum in Illinois in 1998, but could have easily taken place in Ontario in the 1950s.

Opposite: Vintage automobiles and a vintage F7 team up to make a vintage scene at the Monticello Railway Museum in 2000. An active preservation movement in the United States has led to the ability to recreate scenes of bygone times with both steam and diesel locomotives.

Left: In 1943 the Baldwin Locomotive Works produced a 6,000-hp diesel riding on two four-axle powered trucks along with two-axle leading and trailing trucks. The locomotive was unsuccessful, but Seaboard purchased a 3,000-hp version of the locomotive.

Below: These locomotives, riding on 24 wheels, were dubbed "Centipedes." In addition to the Seaboard, the Pennsylvania Railroad and the National Railway of Mexico purchased this model. In all, there were 40 units operating in the U.S. and 14 in Mexico.

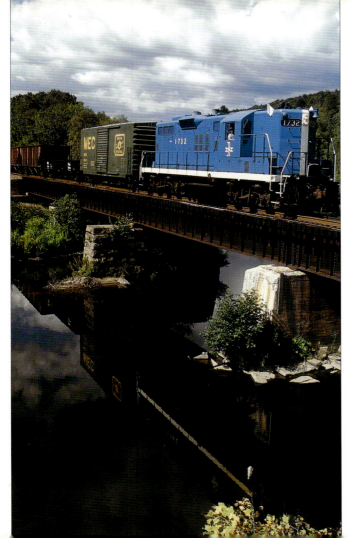

Above: Patterned after the Raymond Loewy-designed body of the 4-4-4-4 T1 steam locomotive, the Pennsylvania Railroad ordered "shark nosed" RF16 diesels from Baldwin in 1949. The Baltimore & Ohio and New York Central also had "sharks" on their rosters. In all, 109 RF16s were constructed between 1950 and 1953. Two survive today.

Left: A GP9 that worked for the Boston & Maine leads a recreated 1950s freight train on the Naugatuck Railway in Connecticut. The GP9 model was introduced by EMD in 1954 and over 4,000 units were produced. Its immediate predecessor, the GP7, had over 3,000 units produced.

While diesel locomotives were being used for switching in the United States, north of the border the first main line diesel was developed. The Canadian Locomotive Company and Westinghouse Electric teamed up on a locomotive (actually two locomotives operating as a back-to-back pair) for Canadian National in 1929. With a Beardsley prime mover adapted from use in submarines, the locomotives proved unreliable.

SPECIFICATIONS

Builder	Canadian National	Wheel Arrange	2-D-1
Tractive Effort	50,000lb (222kN)	Length	47ft 0-1/2in (14,388mm)
Weight	255,644lb (116t)	Max. Axleload	63,920lb (29t)
		Year Built	1929

Canadian National No.9000 arrived on the railroad as two locomotives coupled back-to-back. Following a demonstration period, the two were separated and numbered 9000 and 9001. No.9000 worked until 1939, No.9001 until 1947.

Right: The Union Pacific was the only railroad to make a major investment into gas-powered turbine locomotives. General Electric delivered 56 turbines to UP between 1952 and 1961.

Opposite: A 2,000-hp GP20 produced in 1959 for the Western Pacific joins a 1,750-hp GP9 built for the Southern Pacific in 1955.

Bottom right: The prime mover is lowered into a Missouri Pacific diesel in 1950.

Below: In its first year of service, one of UP's turbines crosses the fly-over in Utah's Echo Canyon in 1954.

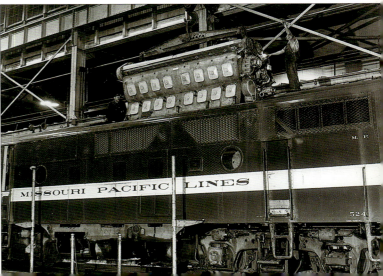

Below: U25B No.2525 was the last locomotive delivered to the New York, New Haven & Hartford before the railroad became a part of Penn Central in 1968. The "U" series was introduced by General Electric with the U25B in 1959. The "B" in U25B indicated the locomive rode on two-axle, or "B"-type, trucks.

Opposite: A pair of U23B's work in the mist at Bucksport, Maine, on Guilford Transportation's Maine Central Railroad. The U23B was introduced by GE in 1968. Guilford Transportation purchased four New England railroads in the 1980s (Maine Central, Boston & Maine, Delaware & Hudson, and Springfield Terminal) and still operates all but the D&H.

Opposite: Burlington Northern C30-7 No.5506 leads a coal train in the Powder River Basin in Wyoming. General Electric discontinued the "U-Boats" in favor of "B" series (four axles) and "C" series (six axle) models in the 1970s. The Powder River Basin is one of the largest coal fields in North America. To tap its resources, one of the largest railroad construction projects of the second half of the 20th Century was completed, with over 100 miles of new track.

Above: The influence of dieselization can be seen in the variety of products that touted the new way to power trains. Toys of sleek modern diesels were made, and railroads put the shiny, clean locomotives on their publicity materials. Also seen in the collection above are builders plates from Baldwin, which had merged with Lima in 1950 (lower left), and newcomer to the locomotive building game, the Electro-Motive Division of General Motors (top center right).

Above: A long intermodal train wraps all the way around the famous Tehachapi Loop in southern California. The Loop is used by trains of Burlington Northern & Santa Fe, and Union Pacific.

Opposite: A revolution in the consist of freight trains occured in the late 20th Century. While freights still run with a mix of boxcars, flat cars, and the like, unit intermodal trains became more and more common, such as this container train.

Left: Intermodal trains could have either containers or highway trailers on flat cars. With a country that spans 3,000 miles, it is more efficient for long-haul trailers to be taken off the highways and put on the railroads.

Profile: F3 Model B-B

Generally regarded as the locomotive that ultimately doomed steam power, the F-series of locomotives from the Electro-Motive Division of General Motors proved to be one of the best-selling series of all time. Starting with the FT in 1939, the ubiquitous locomotives were soon showing up all over the country. The F2 was next, but it was the F3 that led the postwar dieselization blitz. Nearly 2,000 of the locomotives were built between 1945 and 1949. The follow-up F7 proved even more successful, with nearly 4,000 units sold in North America.

SPECIFICATIONS

Builder	General Motors	Wheel Arrange	B-B	
Tractive Effort	57,500lb (256kN)	Length	50ft 8in (15,443mm)	
Weight	230,000lb (104.4t)	Max. Axleload	57,500lb (26.1t)	
		Year Built	1945	

The F3 came in both "cab" and "booster" configurations, and railroads could place as many boosters behind a cab unit as they needed. Cab units were designated "A" units and boosters were "B" units. A cab-booster combination was in "A-B" configuration.

Above: An intermodal train exits Pattenburg Tunnel in New Jersey. The train is destined for the busy terminals near New York City.

Left: A train of double-stacked containers snakes through the Tehachapi mountains.

Right: Intermodal traffic isn't the only traffic moving in intermodal trains. Almost any bulk commodity can move in unit trains, such as coal or grain. A train of tank cars carrying oil snakes through the Tehachapi Mountains. The tank cars are interconnected by piping so that several cars can be loaded from one connection.

Below: All the major North American railroads upgraded clearances in the 1990s to handle double-stacked containers. The containers are lifted off a truck or ship and placed directly into well cars for shipment by rail. Double-stack trains are some of the most impressive trains to view.

Opposite: Another unit train, this one hauling gas, rolls along Montana Rail Link near Paradise, Montana. The train is passing a semaphore signal, a very common type of signal in the mid-20th Century. By the end of the 1990s, only a handful of the trackside sentinels remained, replaced by signals with color lights. The new signals have no moving parts.

Above: The largest diesel locomotives ever built were the DD40AX units purchased from General Motors by Union Pacific. Riding on eight axles, the DD40AX was the last eight-axle diesel produced in North America. No.6936 is the last operating DD40AX, retained by Union Pacific for excursions and other passenger specials.

Above: Coal has always been one commodity that moves in unit trains. A coal train snakes down the Front Range of the Rocky Mountains approaching Denver, on former Denver & Rio Grande Western trackage. Union Pacific now operates the former D&RGW.

Right: An empty coal train departs West Brownsville, Pennsylvania, heading for the Monongahela coal fields. The train has to share the road with highway traffic as it moves through the town. On the head end is a trio of "Super 7s" built by General Electric. in 1972 for the Monongahela Railroad.

Right: With the aspen trees changing colors, a coal train heads towards Moffat Tunnel in the Colorado Rockies. The line was owned by the Denver & Rio Grande Western until it merged with Southern Pacific. Ultimately, SP was purchased by Union Pacific.

Below: No state is more synonymous with coal than West Virginia. Both the Chesapeake & Ohio and Norfolk & Western penetrated the rugged terrain of the "Mountain State." A CSX train rolls on former C&O rails at Alderson.

In 1949 General Motors introduced the GP7 (GP standing for General Purpose and often called "Geeps"), the first model in a long-running series that would culminate with the GP60 in the 1990s. The GP7 was an immediate hit, and it and its immediate successor, the GP9, had 4,157 units sold. The GP9 produced 1,750 hp, but by turbocharging EMD's 567 power plant, the horsepower increased to 2,000 and the GP20 was produced. The GP30 took the horsepower to 2,250, and another 250 hp was added for the GP35. By the time the GP60 was introduced, the 567 power plant had been supplanted, first by the 645 engine and then the 710. GP production had stopped by the year 2000.

SPECIFICATIONS

Builder	General Motors
Tractive Effort	61,000lb (271kN)
Weight	244,000lb (108.9t)
Wheel Arrange	B-B
Length	56ft 0in (17,120mm)
Max. Axleload	61,000lb (27.2t)
Year Built	1949

General Motors of Canada built the GP38-2 locomotive for Canadian Pacific, a model that was also popular with US roads and built by EMD. The "Dash-2" designation reflected upgraded electrical equipment, and other improvements.

Opposite: What appears to be the front of a train is actually the rear. An AC4400 (Alternating Current, 4,400 hp) built by General Electric pushes the rear of a long coal train. Spreading the power between the front and rear of the train reduces the stresses within the train.

Below: The locomotives on a Canadian Pacific westbound coal train pass their caboose on a horseshoe curve in British Columbia.

Above: A Denver & Rio Grande Western coal train rolls through Castle Gate (named for the impressive rock formation in the background) in Utah. The D&RGW was primarily a freight carrier, although it was more famous for its passenger trains.

Right: The Duluth, Missabe & Iron Range hauls taconite pellets from the mines in Minnesota to waiting ore ships that will sail the Great Lakes. With a well-maintained fleet of SD locomotives (including the SD9 model produced between 1954 and 1959), the DM&IR is a good-looking railroad. An empty train heads from Lake Superior back to the mines.

Left: Once the primary source of employment in the eastern Pennsylvania town, Bethlehem Steel's plant is but a shadow of itself as a Conrail train passes in the late 1980s. Within a decade, the plant will be completely closed and this part of Conrail will belong to Norfolk Southern.

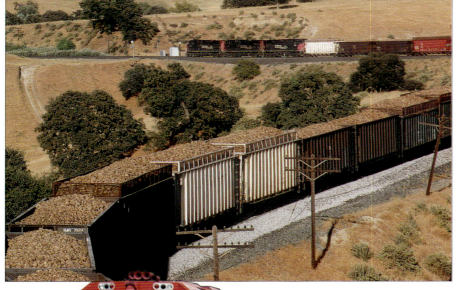

Left: Until the year 2001, sugar beets moved in unit trains from loaders to processing plants in California. The changing nature of the sugar processing business, however, ended the annual appearance of the beet trains and closed most of California's refineries.

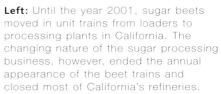

Below: Woodchips move from the forests of British Columbia on the province-owned BC Rail. Leading the train is an SD40-2, one of the most successful models ever designed by General Motors.

Left: Automobiles are loaded onto a Canadian National train. The "auto rack" cars are coupled together in long strings, and the first autos loaded must drive through several of the rail cars. Autos are shipped by rail from the assembly plant to distribution centers, where trucks take over for final delivery.

Below: An empty auto rack train traverses the famed Horseshoe Curve near Altoona, Pennsylvania. Auto racks lacked roofs until the 1990s, when the auto carriers became fully enclosed to minimize vandalism and damage during transit.

Right: With Mount Shasta looking down, a freight rolls north on the Southern Pacific at Andesite, California. These tracks are now owned by Union Pacific. The typical freights of mixed commodities still run, although unit trains are becoming more common. Boxcars and refrigerator cars still carry goods such as paper and produce. Railroads move about 40% of all intercity freight in the United States.

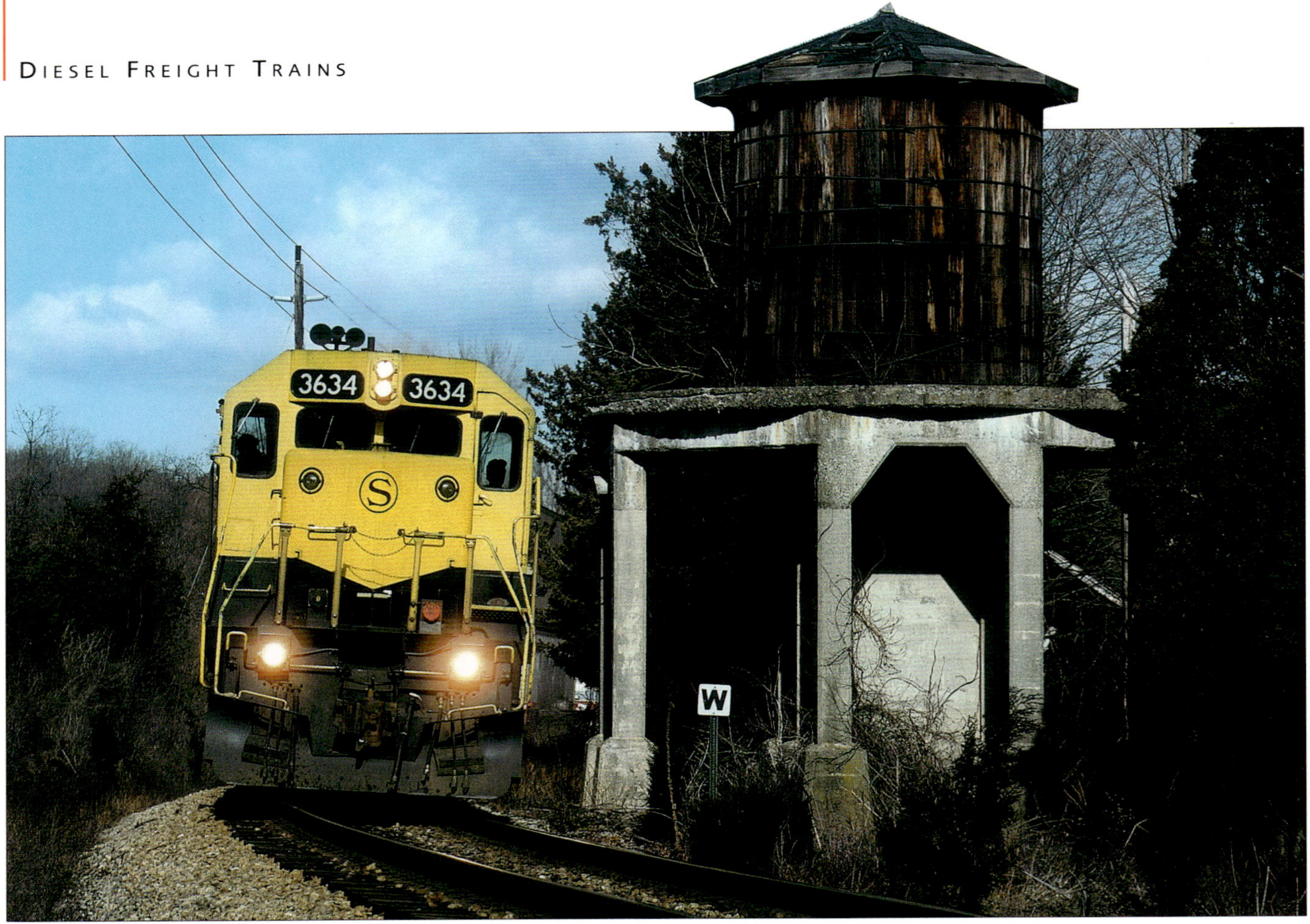
3634
3634
S
W

Opposite: An SD45 leads a freight on the New York, Susquehanna & Western past an anachronism from steam days, the water tank at Sparta Junction, New Jersey. There are still a few steam structures left along the railroads.

Right: Tennessee Pass in Colorado is the highest main line in the United States, crossing the Continental Divide at an altitude of over 10,000 feet. Historically a route of the Denver & Rio Grande Western, the line was taken out of service by successor Union Pacific in 1997.

Left: One of the railroading engineering marvels in the U.S. is Tehachapi Loop in California, a complete circle designed for trains to gain elevation. A downhill Southern Pacific train emerges from the bottom of the Loop while the rear of the train passes overhead.

While the Electro-Motive Division of General Motors was the number one diesel producer in the 1940s and 1950s, the second largest producer was the American Locomotive Company, with electrical components supplied by General Electric. But in the early 1950s, GE broke away from Alco to produce locomotives on its own. GE's answer to the GP-series from GM was the "U-Series" (the "U" meaning universal; the locomotives were often called U-Boats). GE introduced the U25B in 1960, a roadswitcher with 2,500 horsepower. And while the U25B sold 478 units, certainly a respectable number, it was a far cry from the sales GM was racking up with the GP-series.

SPECIFICATIONS	
Builder	General Electric
Tractive Effort	81,000lb (360kN)
Weight	260,000lb (118.0t)
Wheel Arrange	B-B
Length	60ft 2in (18,340mm)
Max. Axleload	65,000lb (29.5t)
Year Built	1960

The U25B was the first mass-produced locomotive built by General Electric after its split from the American Locomotive Company in 1953. With the U25B, GE replaced Alco as the number two builder in the United States.

Left: EMD's most successful model in the "SD" series was the SD40-2, introduced in 1972. Five of the locomotives lead a Union Pacific train on Sherman Hill at Dale Junction, Wyoming, in 1982.

Opposite: Canadian Pacific also used SD40-2s in great quantities. This view is looking forward from a set of six units in the middle of a grain train on Rogers Pass in British Columbia. Four more SD40-2s are ahead out of sight.

Below: An SD40-2 leads a Canadian Pacific freight uphill out of Field, British Columbia, in 1988. CPR had nearly 500 SD40-2s for working almost every freight in western Canada. Union Pacific had almost 1,000 of the units.

Left: Every autumn the grain trains start rolling in Canada. Historically, the cars were loaded at small elevators in many towns along seldom-used branch lines, and gathered into long trains for the main line. Today, grain is gathered at large elevators along main lines, and many branches have been abandoned.

Below: A caboose is at the rear of a Canadian Pacific freight near Swift Current, Saskatchewan. Cabooses were largely replaced by automated telemetry boxes that transmit information to the locomotives. This caboose operating in 2001 was definitely a rare find.

Right: The Anheuser Busch brewery (home of Budweiser) in St Louis, Missouri, uses its own railroad to switch the plant. The Manufacturers Railway moves tank cars and boxcars of raw materials into the brewery to be made into beer, and the finished product leaves the plant in refrigerator cars. This railroad has been in service since 1887, and today operates with a small fleet of switching locomotives purchased from General Motors.

Left: There is no access for freight trains into New York City directly from the west through New Jersey. At one time, most area railroads had marine operations to float rail cars into the city on barges. The last marine railroad in the area is the New York Cross Harbor.

Below: The New York Cross Harbor's barge approaches the pier at Greenville, New Jersey, where freight cars will be loaded for the trip across the harbor to Brooklyn. The first rail bridge over the Hudson River is located near Albany, New York, over 100 miles north of New York City.

Left: Another brewery with its own railroad is the Coors brewery in Golden, Colorado. Concentrated beer is loaded into tank cars in Golden and transported to Virginia, where water is added to make beer for distribution on the east coast of the United States.

Opposite: Some of the finest short line railroading can be found in New England, where grand scenery and friendly railroads abound. A Vermont Railway train approaches the state line on its run from Rutland, Vermont, to Whitehall, New York.

Opposite right: Cape Cod, which protrudes into the Atlantic Ocean off Massachusetts, has a problem—its dense population produces a lot of trash with no place to put it. The Cape Cod Railroad hauls garbage off the Cape in specially sealed containers.

What railroad other than Union Pacific, the railroad that had the Big Boy, would own the largest diesels ever produced? By taking two GP40s and splicing them together, UP had a locomotive that was 98 feet (29,997mm) long. Built in 1969, 100 years after the driving of the golden spike, the big units were given the name "Centennials" and numbered in the 6900 series. From 1969 until 1971 there were 47 DD40AX's constructed by General Motors. These were the last custom-built diesels ordered by the UP.

SPECIFICATIONS

Builder	General Motors	Wheel Arrange	D-D
Tractive Effort	133,766lb (603kN)	Length	98ft 5in (29,997mm)
Weight	525,270lb (247.5t)	Max. Axleload	68,324lb (31.0t)
		Year Built	1969

DD40AX No.6900 was built for the Union Pacific in 1969. All but one of the Centennials have been retired, with No.6936 still in service hauling excursions and special passenger trains for shippers.

Below: A busy rail corridor is the former Richmond, Fredericksburg & Potomac (now CSX) between Washington, D.C., and Richmond, Virginia. Hugging the Atlantic coast line, it crosses numerous rivers and harbors on scenic trestles. This is a busy passenger route, as well.

Opposite: When bad weather strikes and the airports and highways are closed, the railroads keep rolling. A Conrail train emerges from Pattenburg Tunnel in a surprise early spring blizzard on March 31, 1997. Over two feet of snow would accumulate during the storm.

Left: A Norfolk Southern train pulls into West Point, Virginia, home of a large paper mill. NS serves this former Southern Railway branch line from a connection at Richmond, the state's capital.

Below: A slow coal train waits in a siding for a faster auto rack train to pass in the West Virginia mountains.

Opposite: Norfolk Southern was formed by the merging of the Norfolk & Western and the Southern Railway. It later expanded when it split Conrail up with CSX. A softball game goes undisturbed by the passing of an NS train on former Conrail tracks at Lyons, Pennsylvania.

Left: The famous "Rat Hole" line runs south from Cincinnati, Ohio, through Kentucky. The line was named for all the tunnels it once had, most replaced by deep cuts.

Opposite: An ore train heads towards the Great Lakes on the railroad owned by Reserve Mining. Another nearby railroad owned by LTV Steel shut down in 2001.

Right: The steepest main line grade in North America is Saluda Hill, located in North Carolina, with a grade of nearly five percent.

Opposite: Union Pacific No.9511 leads a westbound train at Dale Junction, Wyoming, after a storm has passed. No.9511 is a Dash 8-41CW built by General Electric in 1993. GE went to the rather cumbersome "Dash" model names in 1990. Many railroads call the model a less awkward "C41-8W."

Left: A Canadian National freight doesn't bother to stop at the wooden grain elevator at Ridpath, Saskatchewan. Once numbering in the thousands, hundreds of wooden grain elevators are closed or demolished each year.

Right: Times aren't what they used to be on the Empress Subdivision of Canadian Pacific near Sceptre, Saskatchewan. The daily train that works the branch passes a farm that has seen better days.

Below: The bright lights of Las Vegas, Nevada, illuminate a Union Pacific train in the gambling center's yard. The locomotives are a pair of UP's ubiquitous SD40-2s from General Motors.

Above: A train rolls along the Lucin Cut-Off, a 30-mile-long causeway built across the Great Salt Lake in Utah. Originally built as a timber trestle across the Lake, it was ultimately rebuilt using rock fill. It has been a constant battle to keep the Cut-Off from sinking into the Lake.

Right: The Grangeville Branch of the Camas Prairie Railroad is known as the "railroad on stilts," due to the numerous wooden trestles along the line. The Rock Creek Trestle near Culdesac, Idaho—although impressive—is not the biggest trestle on the line.

Profile: SD-40 C-C

With the success of its four-axle GP-series firmly established, the Electro-Motive Division of General Motors developed a line of six-axle locomotives called the "SD" series (Special Duty). Basically, the SD-series were the same as the GP-series, except six axles meant lighter axle loadings and greater weight (and thus better adhesion). Thus, both GP38 and SD38 models were offered, GP40 and SD40, and so forth. Like the GP-series, the SD's received "Dash-2" designations (such as the SD40-2) when better electrical systems were developed. By the 1990s, all the major US railroads were looking for maximum horsepower, and both GE and EMD ceased producing four-axle locomotives. In fact, GE and EMD were locked in a horsepower race with each other, as both strived to market the first successful 6,000-h.p. locomotive. EMD came up with the SD90MAC, but GE took the locomotive production lead away from EMD for the first time with its AC6000CW.

SPECIFICATIONS

Builder	General Motors	Wheel Arrange	C-C
Tractive Effort	83,100lb (370kN)	Length	68ft 10in (20,980mm)
Weight	368,000lb (167.0t)	Max. Axleload	61,330lb (27.8t)
		Year Built	1972

The SD40-2 was a very popular model in the SD-series, with Conrail, Union Pacific, Canadian Pacific, and others ordering hundreds of copies. The SD40-2 was introduced in 1972, an upgraded version of the popular SD40.

Right: Canadian National SD40-2W (the "W" indicating a wide nose) No.5327 works the freight yard at Lynn Creek, British Columbia, near Vancouver. The SD40-2W's were built by General Motors Diesel Division, the Canadian equivalent of the Electro-Motive Division.

Opposite: A Burlington Northern freight runs along the Columbia River in Washington State. The BN merged with the Atchison, Topeka & Santa Fe in 1995 to form the Burlington Northern & Santa Fe, more commonly called BNSF.

Right: The Southern Pacific's main line from Portland, Oregon, to California passes through the rugged Cascade Mountains. A General Electric Dash 9-44CW leads a train west of Oakridge, Oregon.

Below: A Southern Pacific SD70M leads a train across the Salt Creek Trestle in the Oregon Cascades. The SD70M was built by General Motors and has a horsepower rating of 4,000. SP received their SD70Ms in 1994.

Left: Although primarily a passenger route, the scenic Coast Line between San Francisco and San Diego, California, sees occasional freight trains. A freight runs directly along the Pacific Ocean at San Clemente, California, in 1991. Amtrak operates frequent trains on this line.

Below: "Cowl" units are diesels with full-length wide carbodies, not the far more typical narrow carbodies with walkways. Very few cowl units were in freight service after the retirement of the F's and FA's on most railroads, but an exception was Santa Fe's SDF45s, which were built in 1982.

7

Diesel Passenger Trains

Once the diesel locomotive was making major inroads into the ranks of steam locomotives operating in freight service, the next logical step was to adapt the new motive power for passenger use. Spurred by the streamliner movement after World War II, diesels were soon leading the finest trains in North America.

Left: Western Pacific FP7 No. 913 once led the California Zephyr between Salt Lake City, Utah, and Oakland, California.

Opposite: The Pennsylvania Railroad had a fleet of self-propelled "doodlebugs" to provide passenger service on lightly used branches. No.4662 is typical of the PRR motorcars. It was built in 1929, and is still in tourist service on the Wilmington & Western Railroad in Delaware.

Above: A small passenger-carrying motor car is at Omaha, Nebraska, on April 10, 1905. The car was used by the Union Pacific Railroad.

Right: The Lancaster, Oxford & Southern in Pennsylvania used a motor car to handle its passenger business, which wasn't very substantial. The car was built in 1915 by Sanders and still sees occasional service on the Strasburg Rail Road.

Right: The earliest streamliners were the Zephyrs built for the Chicago, Burlington & Quincy. On May 27, 1934, the first Zephyr made the run from Chicago to Denver, Colorado, in a little over 13 hours, averaging 78 mph for the trip.

Below: As an answer to Burlington's Zephyrs, the Union Pacific and Chicago & North Western teamed up to operate a streamlined train, The City of Portland, between Chicago and Portland, Oregon.

Above: The Zephyr trains carried neon tail signs, letting everyone know which Zephyr passed in the night.

Right: The Pioneer Zephyr was the first of the CB&Q's Zephyrs. The train was a three-car articulated set. Ultimately, the Zephyrs would be powered by more conventional E-units pulling conventional cars.

The Rio Grande Southern had entered Colorado to tap the mineral wealth found in the state, but the narrow gauge line was in for hard times. Filing for bankruptcy in 1929, and looking to cut costs wherever possible, the railroad's receiver, Victor A. Miller, ordered the manufacture of railcars made from automobile parts. In June 1931 the first of these railcars—made from a Buick and designed to haul mail—appeared, and its ungainly waddle as it headed down the tracks led it and its successors to be called "Galloping Geese." Goose No.2 was slightly larger, but when Goose No.3 included seating for twelve passengers, suddenly the Geese could make more money than it cost to run them. No.4 followed in 1932 and No.5 came along in 1933. Both were nearly identical to No.3. The last two Geese were built for special purposes. Goose No.6 was used to move labor and material for railroad maintenance, and Goose No.7 had a refrigerated cargo area. With the loss of the mail contract in 1950, four Geese were modified for tourist service with seating for 20 people. The tourist business lasted one year only, just 1951.

Rio Grande Southern Galloping Goose No.5 was built in 1933. As originally constructed, twelve passengers could ride in the front section with the driver while the rear section carried mail and freight. When the mail contract was not renewed, the rear portion was converted into a 20-passenger sightseeing coach. Four original Geese survive, and Goose No.1 has been recreated.

∞THE GALLOPING GOOSE ∞

SPECIFICATIONS

Builder	Rio Grande Southern	Wheel Arrange	B-B-B
Tractive Effort		Length	43ft 3in (13,183mm)
Weight	14,770lb (6.7t)	Max. Axleload	3,600lb (1.65t)
		Year Built	1933

Right: The Abraham Lincoln operated on the Alton & Southern, a railroad controlled by the Baltimore & Ohio, between Chicago and St Louis. Power for the train was a boxcab diesel built by General Motors in 1935.

Below: General Motors sent an A-B-B-A set of FT's on a nationwide tour to prove that diesels could supplant steam in main line service. Some 20 railroads tested the FT set, and most were convinced that diesels were the way of the future.

Above: A Wabash F7 poses at the Nelson's Crossing passenger station at the Monticello Railway Museum in Illinois.

Right: Canadian Pacific restored F7 No. 1400 for use on the Royal Canadian Pacific luxury train. With CPR's classic heavyweight passenger cars, the RCP is a train right out of the 1940s.

Above: FP7s were slightly longer versions of the (usually) freight-hauling F7. The additional length housed a steam generator for heating passenger cars. Southern painted its FP7s in the line's classic green and gold.

Opposite: Perhaps no paint scheme in North America is as famous as the Santa Fe's "warbonnet" scheme as it appeared on the railroad's F7s. Many children grew up with a Lionel train set painted for Santa Fe's Super Chief.

Right: The primary passenger locomotives developed by General Motors were the "E" series, with the E7 (510 units) and E8 (460 units) being the most popular. Delaware, Lackawanna & Western used E8s on the Phoebe Snow.

Right: Santa Fe introduced the Super Chief as a way to entice riders back to the railroads, as the highways and airlines were taking passengers away. The Super Chief was known as the "Train of the Stars," as Hollywood's elite used the train when traveling to and from Los Angeles.

Below: The classic image of the Super Chief was warbonnet F-units leading a train of stainless steel cars across the desert. The Super Chief survived until the advent of Amtrak on May 1, 1971.

Right: As old F-units were retired, some found new life as "cab cars" on commuter railroads. The units had their traction motors and prime movers removed, but could still control a train by using a locomotive on the opposite end. This arrangement allowed railroads to operate commuter trains in either direction without having to move the locomotive to the other end.

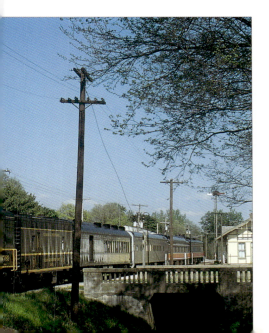

Left: While Alco developed a classic six-axle passenger diesel in the PA, Canadian railroads turned instead to a passenger version of Alco's FA four-axle freight locomotive, the FPA2 and FPA4. Canadian National No.6789, an FPA4, was built by Montreal Locomotive Works in 1959.

Opposite: Waiting for the morning call to work, a line-up of FP9s wait in Dorion, Quebec. Before the sun rises, the veteran cab units—built in 1951 and 1952—will be taking commuters into Montreal. After the sun goes down, the units will be waiting again.

Above: The Maryland Area Rail Commuter agency used their own F9s and a leased CSX FP7 to power its trains between Washington, D.C., and Baltimore and Brunswick, Maryland.

Right: The Montreal Urban Community Transportation Commission used former Canadian Pacific FP9s on passenger trains from Montreal to Dorion, Quebec, over CPR's tracks. Most railroads turned their commuter operations over to government agencies in the 1980s and 1990s.

Below: Union Pacific maintains a small fleet of E-units for excursion and business trains. E9A No.949 sits in Salt Lake City, Utah, in 1997. The next day it will power an excursion for the National Railway Historical Society's annual convention. No.949 was built by General Motors in 1955.

Above: Pennsylvania Railroad E8A No.5706 sits at the shops formerly owned by the Reading Company in Reading, Pennsylvania. The 1950 veteran was restored to its PRR "pinstripe" paint scheme in the 1980s and worked on the Blue Mountain & Reading.

Opposite: The other common Pennsylvania Railroad paint scheme for E-units came with a thick single stripe instead of the five pinstripes. A restored E8A works past MG Tower near Altoona, Pennsylvania, in 2002. The train has just traversed Horseshoe Curve on its climb into the Allegheny Mountains.

In 1930, General Motors purchased the Winton Engine Company. It also purchased Winton's biggest customer, the Electro-Motive Corporation. EMC was quickly transformed into GM's Electro-Motive Division, complete with a new plant in LaGrange, Illinois. The first task at EMD was the design and construction of streamlined diesel locomotives for passenger service. These locomotives operated on "A1A" trucks (three axles, but only the first and third axles being powered; the middle axle was just for weight distribution). In 1930 the Baltimore & Ohio purchased the first E-units, classified as "EA" models. The Santa Fe was the next buyer, picking up a slightly improved model called the E1. The E2 model went to the railroads operating the City of San Francisco and City of Los Angeles streamliners. Following were the E4 model for Seaboard Air Line, the E3 model for Santa Fe, and the E5 for the Chicago, Burlington & Quincy. The E6 became the first mass-produced assembly line diesel for EMD, followed by the extremely successful E7 and E8 models. E-unit production finished with the E9 in 1963.

SPECIFICATIONS

Builder	General Motors	Wheel Arrange	A1A-A1A
Tractive Effort	53,080lb (236kN)	Length	71ft 1-1/4in (21,670mm)
Weight	212,310lb (96.3t)	Max. Axleload	53,080lb (24.1t)
		Year Built	1945

The Chicago, Rock Island & Pacific (usually called simply the "Rock Island") purchased E9 locomotives for its Rocket streamliners. The E9 model only sold 144 units, down from the nearly 500 units of its predecessor, the E8, that had been sold.

Above: The Rock Island's streamliners were known as Rockets. Among the trains operated were the Rocky Mountain Rocket and the Texas Rocket.

Opposite: The United Railroad Historical Society painted a former Pennsylvania Railroad E8 into the colors of the Erie Railroad for excursion service.

Right: A passenger train behind an A-B set of F-units crosses the Baltimore & Ohio's bridge over the Potomac River at Harpers Ferry, West Virginia. The B&O offered frequent service between Baltimore and Washington in the east to Pittsburgh, Chicago, St Louis, and other points west.

Above: New York Central painted its E-units in the famed two-tone gray "Lightning Stripe" scheme. An E9 is seen on the turntable at the Danbury Railway Museum in Connecticut. Interestingly, the NYC never owned E9s (it used primarily E8s), but the museum wanted to show what NYC passenger diesels looked like, so an E9 was used.

Below: Originally intended for passenger service, the Pennsylvania Railroad's Baldwin-built Centipedes were soon demoted to freight duty, and ultimately wound up as helper locomotives pushing freights over the Allegheny Mountains west of Altoona, Pennsylvania. Frequent electrical fires caused by dripping oil led to the downfall of these beasts.

Left: The last great stand for E-units in passenger service was on the former Chicago, Burlington & Quincy main line westward from Chicago, where Metra ran a large fleet of E9s in commuter service. Every evening, dozens of E9-powered trains would depart the Windy City heading for the communities of Hinsdale, LaGrange, Naperville, Lisle, and others.

Above: The former Burlington Northern E9s working for Metra would tie up each night at Aurora, Illinois. The locomotives were originally purchased by the Chicago, Burlington & Quincy between 1953 and 1956 for long-distance passenger service. All the E9s had been retired by the early 1990s, replaced by less stylish FF40PHM-2s built in 1991 and 1992.

Left: When it comes to entertaining shippers or inspecting the right-of-way, there is no better way than the business train. Conrail used a trio of E8s to power its "Office Car Specials." The impressive train passes the Bethlehem Steel plant in Bethlehem, Pennsylvania. With Conrail's break-up by Norfolk Southern and CSX, the E-units were sold.

Opposite: Union Pacific's business train crosses Soldier Summit in Utah in 1997. Union Pacific uses a classy A-B-A consist of E9s, along with a matching set of Armour yellow coaches. The Soldier Summit route was originally part of the Denver & Rio Grande Western.

Opposite right: New York, Susquehanna & Western acquired a pair of ex-Chicago, Burlington & Quincy E9s, retired from Chicago commuter service, to power its business train. The two E-units lead a short train near Oak Ridge, New Jersey.

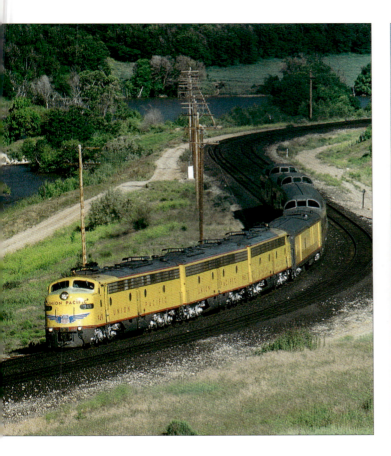

Right: Part of the magic of passenger train travel is the lack of confinement one has on the rails. Unlike on airliners and buses, people can get up to walk around on the train. They might pay a visit to the cafe car for a snack, or the dining car for a delicious meal as the scenery rolls by.

Left: Union Pacific purchased locomotive 50-M-2a in 1945. The locomotive was designed by Fairbanks-Morse and built by General Electric, and was one of three delivered to the UP (two "A" units and a "B" cabless booster unit). Delivered as freight locomotives, the units were regeared to attain higher speeds for passenger service in 1946.

Below: The City of San Francisco was a streamliner that operated over three railroads on its run from Chicago to San Francisco—the Chicago & North Western, Union Pacific, and Southern Pacific. The journey included a ride across the Great Salt lake in Utah on Southern Pacific's Lucin Cut-Off.

Right: Passenger trains offer a variety of sleeping options, from single berths to full bedrooms. Many bedrooms in sleeping cars had two beds, an upper and lower berth. The upper berth folded out from the ceiling when it came time for its use; the lower berth often converted from two chairs that were used during the day.

Profile: Santa Fe Alco PA-A1A

In response to the E-series being produced by General Motors, the American Locomotive Company responded with a six-axle streamlined diesel of its own. The result was the PA1 locomotive, which would generally become known as the greatest passenger diesel locomotive of all time.

The first PA1s rolled out of the shop in September 1949 and 170 "A" cab units and 40 cabless "B" booster units were produced by June 1950. The PA2 followed, with 28 cab units and two booster units produced. Finally, the PA3 was introduced, with 49 cab units and five boosters. PA production ceased in 1953. By the 1970s, only four PAs were left, and these found a home on the Delaware & Hudson. The D&H sold the units to Mexico, and two have been repatriated for restoration in the US.

SPECIFICATIONS

Builder	American Locomotive	Wheel Arrange	A1A-A1A
Tractive Effort	51,000lb (227kN)	Length	65ft 8in (20,015mm)
Weight	306,000lb (138.8t)	Max. Axleload	51,000lb (23.1t)
		Year Built	1946

The PA1 is considered the finest passenger locomotive ever produced, and the paint scheme that brought out the best in them was the Santa Fe's "warbonnet." One of four surviving PA's is being restored for display at the Smithsonian Institution in Washington, DC. A second PA is being restored in Oregon and two are on display in museums in Mexico.

Above:
A timetable touts the advantages of riding the Gulf, Mobile & Ohio through the South.

Opposite: Westinghouse Electric tried to enter the gas-turbine locomotive market with No.4000, constructed in 1950. High operating costs led the unit to be scrapped in 1952.

Right: A Missouri Pacific cab unit undergoes a major shopping in 1940.

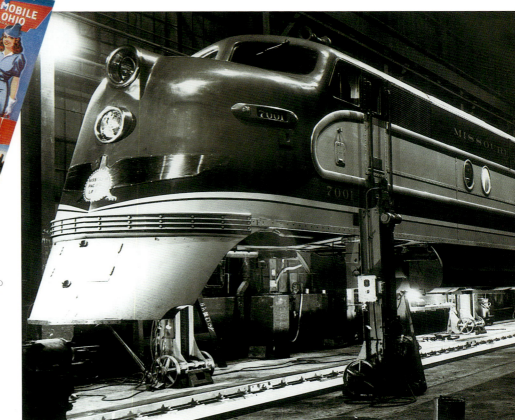

Right: The White Pass & Yukon Route carries tourists from Skagway, Alaska, into British Columbia. In the 1980s the WP&YR was faced with abandonment, but new business from cruise ships saved the railroad.

Below: Two Aerotrains were built by General Motors in 1956, running on various lines before both wound up on the Rock Island. In 1966 both train sets were donated to museums.

Opposite: Many railroads used self-propelled Rail Diesel Cars (RDCs), built by the Budd Company to serve lightly-patronized routes. The Pennsylvania-Reading Seashore Lines used RDCs for its commuter service from Camden, New Jersey, to communities along the Atlantic Ocean. Cape May Seashore Lines now operates ex-PRSL cars over a part of former PRSL trackage.

Right: The New York, New Haven & Hartford purchased 60 unique FL9s for commuter service into Grand Central Terminal. The locomotives were dual powered, operating as diesel locomotives through the Connecticut suburbs, but when they reached the Park Avenue Tunnel in Manhattan, they switched to electric power to avoid diesel fumes in the tunnel. The most famous paint scheme worn by the FL9s was the red, white, and black of the New Haven. When the locomotives became a part of Penn Central and Conrail, they lost their New Haven paint. But when the Connecticut Department of Transportation took over the state's commuter operations in the 1980s, it painted several FL9s back into the classic scheme.

Opposite: Amtrak inherited six FL9s when it took over operating long-distance passenger trains from Penn Central in 1971. The FL9s were assigned to Empire Corridor service between New York City and Albany, New York. The FL9s had a four-axle lead truck and six axle rear truck, unique on diesel power. All FL9s were retired by mid-2002.

Profile: FL9 Bo-Bo-A1A

The New York, New Haven & Hartford Railroad was an electrified line that ran from Grand Central Terminal and Pennsylvania Station in New York City to New Haven, Connecticut. By the late 1950s, the New Haven was considering eliminating its electric power and going strictly with diesels. The only problem was how to deal with the two-mile-long Park Avenue Tunnel under Manhattan or the East River Tunnels. The answer came in the form of the FL9 locomotive. A hybrid, the FL9 could operate as a straight diesel through Connecticut, but when it reached New York it could pick up electricity with shoes attached to the trucks from the electrified "third rail" along the tracks. Between 1956 and 1960, the New Haven received 60 FL9s from General Motors. The New Haven decided to retain its electric infrastructure, but the FL9s proved to be worthy locomotives, able to provide non-electrified branch lines with direct service into New York.

SPECIFICATIONS		Wheel Arrange	B-A1A
Builder	General Motors	Length	59ft 0in (17,983mm)
Tractive Effort	58,000lb (258kN)	Max. Axleload	57,984lb (26.3t)
Weight	231,937lb (105.2t)	Year Built	1956

The FL9s worked for the New Haven until it became part of Penn Central in 1968, and then Conrail in 1976. When Conrail was relieved of operating commuter trains, the FL9s went to work for the Metro-North Commuter Railroad and soon found themselves working on former New York Central lines along the Hudson River. By mid-2002, all FL9s had been retired, some after 40-plus years of service.

Left: An FL9 awaits the call to service at Danbury, Connecticut. The New Haven operated commuter service to its namesake town as well as branches to Danbury, Waterbury, and New Canaan, Connecticut.

Below: The F40PH became the standard passenger locomotive in North America in the 1980s, as both Amtrak and VIA Rail Canada—as well as several commuter agencies—purchased the locomotives. An F40 leads VIA's Canadian at Lake Louise, Alberta.

Right: The Canadian remains the last of the great streamliners in North America. With Budd-built stainless steel coaches and a classy dome-observation car at the rear, the train is a throwback to the 1950s. Historically operating over the Canadian Pacific, the train now passes through the Rocky Mountains on Canadian National's route.

Left: One of the most unusual trains to operate in North America was Ontario Northland's TEE (Trans-European Express) train set. With a very European look, the train operated northward out of Toronto. The original power car that propelled the train was replaced by an F7, but the odd-looking cab car was retained.

Opposite: At the Race Street engine terminal in Philadelphia is an impressive line-up of Amtrak passenger power. At the left is an E60CH electric locomotive, next to an F40PH diesel. In the center is a Virginia Railway Express GP35-2C leased by Amtrak. Next is a GP7 used by Amtrak for work train service, and at the right is a New Jersey Transit F40PH-2CAT for Atlantic City service.

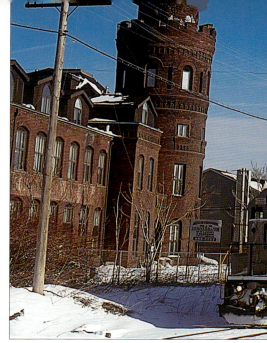

Left: Sometimes freight locomotives get to power passenger trains. A Chessie System (now CSX) GP40, still wearing the colors of predecessor Baltimore & Ohio, leads a National Railway Historical Society convention excursion through Ohio en route to Cincinnati from Columbus in 1984.

Above: A New Jersey Transit GP40PH-2 kicks up snow at North Newark, New Jersey, as it heads from Hoboken to Hackettstown. NJT operates commuter service on routes originally run by the Pennsylvania, Jersey Central, Erie, and Lackawanna Railroads; this is a former Erie line.

Right: Leased Caltrain commuter cars wait at the station in San Diego, California, as part of an Amtrak San Diegan train. This former Santa Fe line still sees a substantial number of passenger trains, including Amtrak, and Metrolink and Coaster commuter trains.

End of the day — a New Jersey Transit commuter train soars across Moodna Viaduct near Salisbury Mills, New York, as the sun slowly sets in the west. This train started in Hoboken, New Jersey, directly across the Hudson River from New York City. Commuters leaving Manhattan either rode the PATH light rail trains under the Hudson or a ferry boat across the water to reach Hoboken before boarding the train. This train's run will terminate in Port Jervis, New York, some 70 miles from Hoboken. The route was at one time the main line of the Erie Railroad, but has been downgraded since Conrail took over the Erie's freight trains. In addition to the NJT commuter trains, only an occasional freight will use these rails.

8

Working on the Railroads

Railroads are more than technology and machinery: they are also about people. Starting with the boyhood hero—the engineer—up to the men and women who dispatch the trains and maintain the tracks, it is people who are the heart and soul of the railroad.

Left: While technology has made the job easier, it still takes a track crew to replace worn out rails.

Above: The railroad has always been about people and machinery. The powerful driving wheels couldn't move a single car without the care and guidance of the men and women who work on the railroad.

Left: Steam locomotives are labor intensive machinery, always in need of tender loving care. It was the duty of the engineer to keep his iron steed lubricated properly. The tradition continues today on preserved steam, such as at Steamtown National Historic Site in Scranton, Pennsylvania.

Below: No.90, a 2-10-0 working on the Strasburg Rail Road in Pennsylvania, gets a shot of grease on its running gear before leaving the engine servicing area in the morning. No.90 originally hauled sugar beets in Colorado.

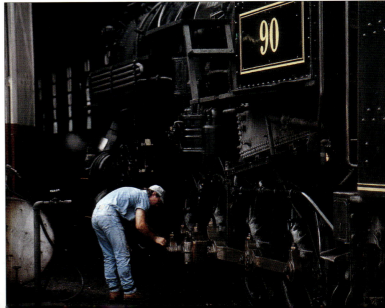

Profile: Engine Crew Gear

During the first half of the 20th Century it was every American boy's dream to be a locomotive engineer. The glamour of having a powerful locomotive and long train all under the control of your right hand certainly was appealing. But working on an engine crew was a lot of work. Until the invention of the stoker, which automatically took coal from the tender and placed it in the firebox, the fireman would have to shovel literally tons of coal each day. Even with a stoker, the fire had to be manually trimmed by the fireman, adding a little coal to places the stoker couldn't reach. The engineer had to walk around the locomotive oiling dozens of lubricators and valves to keep the running gear working smoothly. And if a mechanical problem occurred while on the road, the locomotive crew had to make as good repairs as they could until the locomotive could reach the next roundhouse or shop.

The engineer and fireman wore coveralls, gloves, and long sleeve shirts in the hot locomotive cabs, even on the hottest days—the clothing kept the heat off their skin. The fireman had a scoop for putting coal on the fire. The fireman also used the broom, sweeping the cab floor of coal dust whenever he had a free moment. A variety of wrenches were kept on hand for repairs on the road, and flags and lanterns were used for signalling. Oil cans were used in lubrication, and cotton "waste" (stringy cloth) was used to wipe down surfaces. It may have seemed glamourous, but it was work.

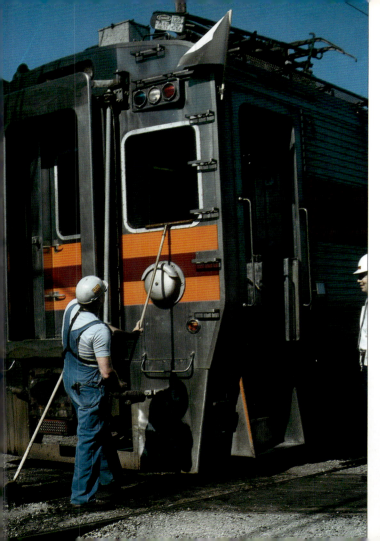

Left: Western Maryland 2-8-0 No.734 takes a long drink of water from a water plug in Cumberland, Maryland, on the Western Maryland Scenic Railroad. Water plugs and water tanks were common sights along the tracks in steam days.

Opposite: A commuter car gets a window washing at the shops of the Chicago, South Shore & South Bend in Michigan City, Indiana.

Below: The locomotive crew would give its locomotive a good wipedown with cotton waste. Special care was given to cleaning the glass on the headlight.

Below: Major railroads are broken up into divisions and subdivisions. When a train reaches the end of a division it will usually get a new crew. An engineer and fireman prepare to board a Union Pacific freight at Green River, Wyoming. Division points were set at every 100 miles in the early days of railroading, as union rules required paying overtime on runs of over 100 miles.

Right: It's early morning and the eastbound road freight on the Cape Breton & Central Nova Scotia is arriving at Stellarton, Nova Scotia, from Truro. A new crew will board here and finish the run to Sydney.

Above: On the East Broad Top, an engineer keeps careful watch as he backs his train through the railroad's yard at Orbisonia, Pennsylvania. The engineer is watching for hand signals from his brakeman. Radios have largely replaced the use of hand signals.

Right: Keeping a hungry steam locomotive fed is the job of the fireman. It is not uncommon for a fireman to shovel tons of coal into the firebox during a run. This fireman is working on a restored 2-8-0 at the North Carolina Transportation Museum.

Below: The Strasburg Rail Road maintains a handsome stable of steam power, including former Norfolk & Western 4-8-0 No.475. The steam locomotives are used in tourist passenger service, but occasionally get out to move the odd freight car the railroad receives. While operating a snow plow train, the engineer and fireman keep a careful watch.

Profile: Railway Maintenance Rig

The job of maintaining track fell to the section gangs, with each gang responsible for anywhere from ten to 25 miles of track, depending on the terrain and how much traffic the line carried. It isn't easy performing maintenance on a busy main line when you have to keep getting out of the way of passing trains. Major jobs required shutting the railroad down for a few hours, giving dispatchers nightmares as trains backed up on either side of the trackwork. But the maintenance needed to be done, and sometimes you just had to stop the trains. The old-time section gangs were made up of strong men called "gandy dancers." They would replace rails, drive spikes, dig out old crossties, tighten bolts, and manicure the right-of-way, all with hand tools. It was back-breaking work, and low paying as well. During the 20th Century, however, more and more maintenance duties became mechanized, and fewer men could cover more miles. Machines were created that could replace track—they would lift up the old rail, remove the old ties, put down new ties, spike the new rail in place, and tamp the ballast without a single man lifting a hammer. A common practice today is for a railroad to do a maintenance "blitz," where many miles of track on one line is replaced or rebuilt all at once. Usually during a maintenance blitz, rail traffic is completely curtailed for several hours each day for weeks on end, with traffic either rerouted or delayed.

Opposite: Among the tools used by "gandy dancers" were pickaxes, shovels, rakes (capable of raking ballast), clamps for lifting rails and ties, wrenches, and hammers. Often, when many men were required to do a single job such as lift a piece of rail, the foreman would lead the men in song and the lifting would occur in time with the music. These chants have all but vanished with the advent of mechanized track maintenance, but the Buckingham Lining Bar Gang—a group of former railroad track workers—still goes to festivals and fairs to show the public what it was like to maintain railroads before machines.

Right: An engineer and fireman work in the cab of a modern diesel locomotive. Today's cabs feature comfortable chairs like you would find in a motor home, as well as microwave ovens, a hot plate for heating water, and a cooler. Electro-Motive introduced the "isolated" cab in the 1990s—a cab that was separated from the rest of the locomotive by sound proofing and shock absorbers. Comforts in the cab have come a long way since the days of hot, dusty steam locomotives.

Left: An engineer in an Amtrak Dash 9-P42B uses the radio to talk to the dispatcher. Modern diesel locomotives have desk-top controls, where the throttle and gauges are arranged as if the engineer was working at a desk somewhere, rather than in a cab.

Opposite: Dormitory cars were used to house the workers constructing what was to become the Great Northern. This scene was typical of railroad construction during the 1880s.

Left: A construction crew pauses for a group portrait while at work on the Seaboard Air Line. The SAL connected Richmond, Virginia, with points in Florida.

Right: Steam locomotives were sometimes prone to starting trackside fires in dry conditions, due to the burning embers that would sometimes fall out of the smokestack and land while still hot. The Southern Pacific had a fire train that patrolled the Sierra Nevada mountains in the 1920s.

Below: The only war fought on US soil in the railroad era was the Civil War between 1861 and 1865. Both the Union and the Confederacy tried to inflict damage on each other's lines to cripple supply routes. Once damaged, the lines were rapidly repaired to keep supplies moving.

Above: Gandy dancers lay track in Missouri the old fashioned way—with hand tools and elbow grease. It took coordination to move a rail, and often the gang would sing to synchronize the work with the beat.

Opposite: A crane removes ties from a cart during a bridge re-decking project. Railroads are responsible for maintaining their own bridges and tunnels—a massive undertaking on some lines.

Right: Track "speeders" were a motorized version of the traditional hand car used to move workers along the railroad and to inspect track. The speeder has been replaced by the "hi-rail" truck, a standard pick-up truck with railroad wheels mounted on it.

Above: Two important documents for a labor union member working for the railroad were his seniority roster and time book. Seniority was an important benefit of being a union member, as it allowed workers with the most years of employment to "bid" on better jobs. Any engineer, conductor, or other union member could "bump" an employee with less seniority from any job within the same craft; likewise, an employee could be "bumped" from a position if someone with more seniority decided he wanted that job. The time book was important in keeping track of an employee's hours, and specific duties performed. Union rules defined most positions in very specific terms, and if an employee was needed to perform a duty outside those terms, he could easily get a full day's pay for five minutes of work outside his specified duties. Some employees made it an art to come home with over two day's pay for only eight hours of work.

Below: The first railroad employee union was formed in 1863 when the engineers of the Michigan Central formed the Brotherhood of the Footboard (later to become the Brotherhood of Locomotive Engineers). Soon most railroad positions had a union group representing them, and most became affiliated with the American Federation of Labor. The first nationwide railroad strike occurred in 1922.

Profile: Conductor's Outfit and Gear

While it was the engineer of a high-speed passenger train who got the awe-filled looks from young boys dreaming of a job on the rails, it was actually the conductor who had all the power. The train was his responsibility, and the engineer could not move the locomotive an inch until the conductor gave him permission. The conductor was (and still is) responsible for the safety of passengers, signalling departures from stations at the appropriate scheduled time, and a myriad of other duties. On long passenger trains, the conductor is often assisted by "trainmen," who dress in uniforms similar to a conductor and share in the responsibility of keeping passengers safe and comfortable (but trainmen have no authority to grant movement of the train). Freight trains usually have conductors as well, but on freights there are no passengers to tend to, so conductors wear regular work clothes. But despite the lack of a uniform, the conductor still controls the train.

The conductor dressed in a uniform, usually a dark blue or black in color. Among the items he carried were a watch set to precise time, an official timetable, tickets, and a ticket punch and a rulebook. Also used were a variety of flags and lanterns for signalling, keys to unlock coaches, or switches and flares for emergency use. Today, a conductor would also carry a radio for communicating with the engineer.

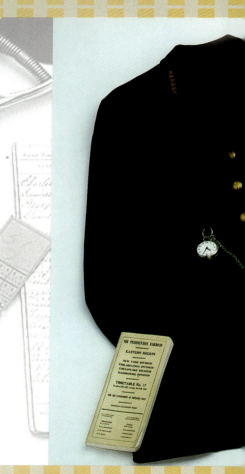

Opposite left: In the days before radio and telegraph communications, it was strict adherence to the timetable that prevented trains from colliding. Trains were supposed to be at a specific place at a specific time, and couldn't proceed beyond that point until all opposing trains had been accounted for. It was critical for every member of the train crew to have an accurate watch for keeping time, and engineers and conductors would check their watches with official railroad clocks at stations and division points.

Opposite right: An Amtrak conductor gives the highball to the engineer. In moments, this train will be on its way eastward from Antioch, California. Passenger trains are usually manned by a conductor and one or more trainmen, whose duties include taking tickets from passengers and opening doors. But the conductor alone has control over the train the engineer cannot move the locomotive until the conductor says he can.

Right: One of the most dangerous jobs in railroading was riding the roofs of cars to set brakes when the train needed to descend a steep grade. The brakemen would have to walk the tops of the swaying cars, using the brake wheel on each car to set the brakes to slow the train's descent and prevent a runaway. Modern air brake technology has made riding the tops of cars a practice that is no longer necessary.

Below: Items used by train crews ranged from the crude to the elegant. The link-and-pin coupler (lower left) required a crew man to stand between cars and manually align the "link" into the pocket, then drop the pin to secure it, all while the train was backing up. This resulted in lost fingers at best, and crushed crewmen at worst. Meanwhile, the elegance of fine silver in the parlor cars was in striking contrast to the dangerous conditions outside the car.

Opposite: Among the tools used by train crews are lanterns for signalling at night, flags for signalling during daylight, locks for switches and the keys to unlock them, ticket punches, an official railroad watch, and a canister of flares for warning trailing trains of danger. Lanterns were orginally illuminated by kerosene-soaked wicks, but battery powered lanterns replaced kerosene in the 1960s.

Right: Heavy repairs to locomotives are performed in shops. A modern diesel shop includes pits for working under locomotives, a drop pit to remove wheels, and cranes that are capable of lifting a locomotive's prime power plant or even an entire locomotive. Most large railroads had only one or two major shops along the system; minor repairs were done at roundhouses at each division point.

Profile: Telegrapher's Office

In the early days trains were dispatched by timetable authority. Train "A" had to be at a certain point at a certain time, and couldn't proceed further until Train "B," which was due at the same point at roughly the same time, had passed. But what if Train "B" was late? Train "A" would sit, making both trains late. One day a railroad official riding on a passenger train was perplexed at the tardiness of a train that was to be met at a station. Entering the station, he asked the telegraph operator to find out if the second train had arrived at the next station down the line. After a few clicks on the keys, the operator said that the train had not arrived there yet. The official then instructed the telegraph operator to tell the station master at the next station to hold the train there until the official's train had arrived. The passenger train then proceeded to the next station, where the process was repeated until the two trains met safely several stations down the line. A lengthy delay to a passenger train had been avoided, and dispatching by telegraph had been born. The telegraph would eventually give way to radio communications and ultimately to computerized dispatching, but dispatching largely remains unchanged from that fateful day when the telegraph was first used. People now control train movements by talking directly to train crews or by setting lineside signals that tell crews when it is safe to proceed.

Opposite: The telegrapher's office included writing desks and instruments for transcribing incoming messages, and telegraph keys for sending messages. Usually located near the stationmaster's office, the telegrapher kept activity at the station flowing smoothly by letting the agent know what trains were on-time, what trains were delayed, and when trains could be expected to arrive.

Above: Locomotives are maintained in shops where heavy repairs can be performed. This Soo Line shop is located in Bensenville, Illinois.

Right: When traveling by train, baggage can be checked just as it is on airplanes today. A typical scene, this one recreated at the Whippany Railway Museum in New Jersey was of handlers loading the baggage car with mail, milk, and travel cases.

Below: Modern dispatching on major railroads is now done from a central control center. Here, dispatchers communicate with trains, sometimes more than 1,000 miles away. Prior to centralized dispatching, control towers located every few miles along the main line would handle train movements, with each tower operator "handing off" each train to the next tower down the line. Today's dispatching centers resemble a space mission control center.

Above: As telegraph and radio communications came into general use on the railroads, the dispatcher was given the authority to control train movements. By communicating directly to train crews, the dispatcher could set up meets at passing sidings on single-track railroads, grant authority for a train to depart a station before a scheduled meet occurs (and holding the other train at a different location), and generally keep the railroad flowing smoothly.

9

Electric Trains

First developed as an alternative to smoke-producing steam locomotives in big cities, electrification on North American railroads was basically limited to a few high-density passenger corridors and even fewer freight lines. As the 21st Century arrived, Amtrak's Northeast Corridor between Boston and Washington was the longest stretch of electrified track on the continent. Cities such as New York, Philadelphia, Montreal, and Chicago also had electrified commuter operations.

Left: An electrified commuter train prepares to head for Montreal at Deux Montagnes, Quebec.

Left: New York Central No.6000 was the first electric loccomotive purchased by the railroad. It was used to power passenger trains through the two-mile-long Park Avenue Tunnel into Grand Central Station (later Terminal). No.6000 was built in 1904 and was followed by 34 other Class "S" electrics. Many operated until the 1970s.

Below: To enter New York City, the Pennsylvania had to tunnel under the Hudson River to the west and the East River to the east. It developed the DD1 electric locomotive in 1909, and they handled all passenger trains into Manhattan until 1924.

Above: The New York, New Haven & Hartford had several electrified lines including the main line between Grand Central Terminal and New Haven, Connecticut. The EP1 locomotive was developed in 1906 to power the New Haven's trains.

Right: Electrified freight operations were much more common in the early 1900s than they are today. California had several electrified lines, including the Tidewater Southern, Central California Traction, and Sacramento Northern. A recreated Sacramento Northern train is seen at the Western Railway Museum in Rio Vista, California.

Above: The Yakima Valley Transportation Company—a subsidiary of Union Pacific—operated freight and trolley service around the town of Yakima, Washington. No. 298 was built by Baldwin-Westinghouse in 1907. The railroad ran trolleys until the 1940s and freight into the 1990s. Today, it is preserved and runs streetcars for tourists.

Left: One route out of Central Station in Montreal requires traversing the three-mile-long Mount Royal Tunnel. To minimize fumes in the tunnel, diesel-powered trains such as Budd Rail Diesel Cars are towed by an electric locomotive to the end of the tunnel.

Below: Montreal's commuter line to Deux Montagnes, Quebec, was a rolling museum into the 1990s. Boxcab electrics built in 1914 faithfully served until 1995, when the line was rehabilitated and new equipment placed in service.

The most ambitious electrification in the western half of North America was the Milwaukee Road's 658 miles of wired track. In 1917 the line between Harlowton and Avery, Montana, was electrified, followed by a segment from Othello to Tacoma, Washington, in 1919. The Milwaukee was the last transcontinental railroad to be built, and as such it had the most difficult profile to negotiate. The most famous locomotives constructed for serving the electrification were the "Bi-Polars," with the first being delivered in 1919 from builder General Electric. The Milwaukee electrification lasted until 1973, when diesels took over all freights on the route. The Milwaukee's entire western extension, the last to be built, was the first to be abandoned when all operations ceased in 1980.

SPECIFICATIONS

Builder	General Electric	Wheel Arrange	2-B-D-D-B-1
Tractive Effort	123,500lb (549kN)	Length	76ft 0in (23,165mm)
Weight	457,000lb (207t)	Max. Axleload	38,500lb (17.5t)
		Year Built	1919

The Milwaukee Road's EP-2 Bi-Polar electrics featured a remarkable 32 driving wheels under the cylindrical body. They operated on 3,000 volts of direct currrent. Only one of the EP-2s—No.E-2—has been preserved.

Above: The most classic of all electrics were the Pennsylvania's GG1 Class locomotives. With an all-welded carbody designed by Raymond Loewy, the GG1 became the most widely-recognized electric in the country, thanks to a very popular Lionel train set.

Below: The GG1 was first introduced in 1934, and by 1943 there were 139 of them working the Pennsylvania's electrified lines. Most of the GG1s survived to work for Penn Central, before being scattered to Conrail, Amtrak, and New Jersey Transit. The last GG1 was retired in 1982.

Above: New Jersey Transit acquired several GG1s and painted No.4877 into the colors of the Pennsylvania Railroad. It powered the last NJT train to be hauled by a GG1 in 1982.

Right: GG1s remained in freight service for Conrail after the carrier was formed in 1976, although Conrail discontinued electric operations shortly therafter. GG1 No.4822 kicks up snow at Princeton Junction, New Jersey, in January 1978.

Opposite: A commuter train for the Southeastern Pennsylvania Transportation Authority (SEPTA) approaches 30th Street Station moments after leaving center city Philadelphia. SEPTA operates a variety of commuter routes out of the city, on trackage once owned by both the Pennsylvania and Reading Railroads. Most service is provided by multiple-unit electric cars—self-propelled cars that require no locomotive.

Above: The Metroliner was the first attempt at high-speed passenger service in the Northeast. Ordered by the Pennsylvania Railroad, the cars entered service after the Penn Central merger in 1967. Amtrak took over the Metroliners along with all other inter-city passenger trains in 1971.

Right: Ready for the evening rush hour, a group of multiple-unit cars of the Chicago, South Shore & South Bend are ready to leave Randolph Street Station in the Windy City. The CSS&SB operates from Chicago to South Bend, Indiana.

10

Rebirth of the Railroads

In the 1980s, North America's railroads made a dramatic turnaround from woeful times in the 1960s and 1970s. Mergers created four major US railroads, dozens of short lines were serving smaller markets, and passenger trains were getting faster.

Left: An Amtrak Turbo train sails along the shores of the Hudson River in New York State.

Left: As the major railroads cut unprofitable branch lines, many of these routes were taken over by short lines. A Canadian American Railway train travels over trackage discarded by Canadian Pacific.

Below: As mergers swallowed up railroads, the power from "fallen flags" could be found all over the new owner's system. A pair of Chicago & North Western locomotives—which had only operated in the plains—trail power from new owner Union Pacific in Utah's Echo Canyon.

Above: To provide power on long, heavy grain trains, railroads like Canadian Pacific employed "Distributed Power Units" (DPUs), which operated in the middle of trains to assist with the load. DPUs are remotely operated from the lead locomotives.

Below: Containers became a huge commodity for railroads in the 1980s and 1990s. These boxes could be easily transported by rail, ship, or truck, so cargo could be loaded in Asia, sail across the Pacific on a ship, be transferred to rail in the US, move across the country by train, and then be transferred to a truck for delivery to its final destination—all without the cargo ever having to leave the container.

Above: A "double-stack" train (containers stacked two high) heads into the setting sun on Union Pacific's Sherman Hill in Wyoming. A constant parade of stack trains crosses the US every day.

Opposite: Double-stack trains also move across Canada— as evidenced by eastbound containers on the prairie of Saskatchewan at Herbert. "Well cars" hold the containers, with the bottom container riding just inches above the rails, allowing enough overhead clearance to stack the containers two-high.

Below: Amtrak was formed in 1971 to relieve the US railroads of unprofitable passenger trains. An F40PH leads a southbound train past the Washington Monument in the nation's capitol.

Above: Amtrak restored service to the new gambling mecca of Atlantic City, New Jersey, in 1989. Alas, the new passenger service couldn't compete with casino-subsidized buses, and Amtrak discontinued service after a few short years. New Jersey Transit still provides commuter service between Atlantic City and Philadelphia.

Right: Despite an 18-inch snowstorm, Amtrak's Lake Shore Limited presses on towards Boston as it passes through Palmer, Massachusetts.

Profile: F40PH B-B

For most of Amtrak's 30-plus years of existence, its workhorse locomotive was the F40PH, built by the Electro-Motive Division of General Motors.

First introduced in 1976, it wasn't long before the F40PH was at the head of practically every non-electrified Amtrak train in the United States. The design was so successful that many commuter railroads were soon ordering F40s as well. Among the cities with F40s in commuter service were New York (New Jersey Transit), Chicago (Metra), Toronto (GO Transit), and San Francisco (Caltrain). By the late 1990s, however, Amtrak's F40 fleet was aging, and replacements were purchased from General Electric in the form of P40s and P42s. Slowly, the F40 fleet dwindled until by early 2002 there were none left in regular service for Amtrak (meanwhile, the commuter F40s continued to roll off the miles). Some Amtrak F40s found new homes in other passenger service, while a few were converted into freight locomotives.

SPECIFICATIONS

Builder	General Motors	Wheel Arrange	B-B
Tractive Effort	68,440lb (304kN)	Length	52ft 0in (15,850mm)
Weight	232,000lb (105.2t)	Max. Axleload	58,000lb (26.3t)
		Year Built	1976

Amtrak 362 was typical of the over 200 F40PH's built by General Motors for the US passenger carrier between 1976 and 1981.

Opposite left: The first power purchased by Amtrak to supplement the aging F40 fleet were 20 Dash 8-P32s purchased from General Electric in 1991. These locomotives were generally confined to California service. The units were dubbed "Pepsi Cans," as they shared similar colors and markings to the soft drink containers.

Opposite: Amtrak also purchased 50 F59PHI locomotives from General Motors beginning in 1994. These streamlined locomotives were used exclusively on Amtrak's expanding California operations. F59PHI No.2007, purchased in 1994, rolls through Jack London Square in Oakland, California.

Right: It was the introduction of the P40-8 and P42-9 units from General Electric that finally ended the F40's reign as Amtrak's primary power. Nearly 200 of the sleek locomotives were purchased beginning in 1993. A new GE and an old F40 lead the California Zephyr through a short tunnel in the Front Range of the Rocky Mountains in Colorado.

Above: The Massachusetts Bay Transportation Authority purchased 55 F40s in different configurations for commuter service in Boston.

Above left: VIA Rail Canada also jumped on the F40 bandwagon, with 59 F40PH-2 locomotives supplementing its aging fleet of General Motors and Montreal cab units.

Opposite: Some very fine railroad museums were established in the 1980s and 1990s. One of the finest is Steamtown National Historic Site in Scranton, Pennsylvania.

Left: Amtrak F40 No.341 makes an international station stop at Niagara Falls, Ontario. The train is the Maple Leaf, operating between Toronto and New York City.

Opposite: Steamtown's grand opening in 1995 drew thousands of people to the new national park in Scranton, Pennsylvania. Guest locomotives—including 4-6-2 No.425 of the Reading, Blue Mountain & Northern—participated in a parade of steam on the park's opening day.

Right: Union Pacific continues its commitment to steam, using it for public relations purposes. The railroad maintains a modern steam shop in Cheyenne, Wyoming, where Northern No.844 and Challenger No.3985 are kept in top-notch shape.

By the late 1970s, VIA's fleet of F-units and FA-units inherited from Canadian National and Canadian Pacific was wearing out. In addition to the F40PH locomotives ordered from General Motors, VIA also ordered twelve LRC (Light, Rapid, Comfortable) locomotives and trainsets from the Montreal Locomotive Works, starting in 1980. Low-slung, the trainsets could negotiate curves at faster speeds than conventional passenger equipment, and the LRC's were assigned to the busy Toronto-Montreal-Ottawa corridor.

The reliability of the LRC's left something to be desired, however, and they seemed to be out of service almost as much as they were in service. Designed to shave 45 minutes off the Montreal-Toronto schedule, they never quite lived up to that potential, as heavy freight traffic on the same line more often than not slowed the quick passenger trains.

SPECIFICATIONS

Builder	Montreal Locomotive	Wheel Arrange	B-B
Tractive Effort	Not available	Length	66ft 5in (202,692mm)
Weight	185,135lb (84.0t)	Max. Axleload	46,285lb (21.0t)
		Year Built	1982

VIA's LRC locomotives were substantially shorter than conventional passenger power, allowing for higher speeds in curves.

Left: Many of VIA's discarded FPA4 locomotives were acquired by tourist railroads and began a third life (after working for VIA and Canadian National). The Napa Valley Wine Train operates one of the finest dinner trains in the US, behind Canadian-built FPA4s.

Above: Short lines took over many lines that the large railroads couldn't operate at a profit. These new railroads used smaller crews and second-hand power to cut costs.

Right: General Motors designed the SD90/43MAC in the late 1990s, featuring a prime mover that could be replaced to produce more horsepower.

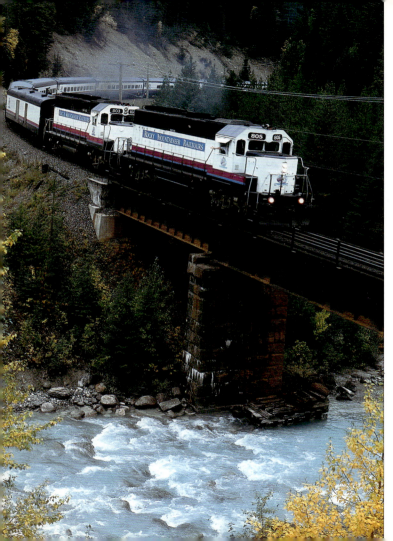

Above: The luxury passenger train made a comeback in the 1990s—but not for business travel. These luxury trains offer "rail cruises" through spectacular scenery. The Alaska Railroad operates a train that is shared by three cruise ship operators between Fairbanks and Anchorage.

Opposite: An Alaska Railroad train drops passengers on the cruise ship dock at Seward, Alaska, as ships for Royal Caribbean and Holland America wait to depart. Cruise ship operators provide tours of Alaska's interior by attaching their own private cars to the rear of the Alaska Railroad's train.

Left: One of the most successful "rail cruise" trains is the Rocky Mountaineer. Departing from Vancouver, British Columbia, the train operates through the spectacular Thompson and Fraser River Canyons, before reaching Kamloops. From there, the train is split for the run through the Rocky Mountains to Jasper and Edmonton in Alberta.

Left: Doing what it was designed to do, a VIA Rail Canada LRC trainset negotiates a curve at high speed. The coaches were equipped with "tilt" technology, where the cars actually tilted in curves to counteract centrifugal forces. Alas, while the coaches worked just fine, the LRC locomotives were subject to mechanical problems.

Right: In 1999 Conrail was sold to rivals CSX and Norfolk Southern, with each railroad acquiring roughly half. A Norfolk Southern train crosses the Susquehanna on the former Conrail (and Pennsylvania) Rockville Bridge.

Opposite: Among the lines acquired by CSX from Conrail was the former New York Central route along the Hudson River. A CSX train heads south in the shadow of Bear Mountain in New York State.

Profile: Class AEM7 B-B

When Amtrak inherited the passenger operations in the Northeast Corridor from PennCentral on May 1, 1971, it inherited GG1 locomotives that had been in service for nearly four decades. It would be another four years, however, before Amtrak would attempt to replace the GG1s.

The first attempt was the boxy E60CP from General Electric. Although long and powerful, tracking problems at high speeds kept the E60s from replacing the GG1s on most New Haven-to-Washington trains. It wouldn't be until 1980, when Amtrak received the first of its AEM7s from General Motors, that a successor to the GG1 was found. Based on the Swedish Rc4 locomotive, the short AEM7s were quickly nicknamed "Swedish meatballs" by Amtrak's shop forces and rail enthusiasts. Amtrak ultimately ordered 47 AEM7s, and they became the standard power on the Northeast Corridor. It wasn't until 2001, with the delivery of HHP8 locomotives and Acela train sets, that the AEM7 would be taken off the fastest trains on the Corridor.

The AEM7 packs a lot of horsepower into a short body. The locomotives are ideally suited for quick acceleration with light passenger trains.

SPECIFICATIONS

Builder	General Motors/ASEA
Tractive Effort	53,300lb (236kN)
Weight	199,500lb (90.6t)
Wheel Arrange	B-B
Length	51ft 5-3/4in (15,700mm)
Max. Axleload	53,300lb (24.0t)
Year Built	1980

Below: Union Pacific methodically acquired several railroads in the 1980s and 1990s, putting its Armour yellow power into places such as Dunsmuir, California, a division point on the former Southern Pacific. In addition to the SP, the UP also acquired the Missouri Pacific, Western Pacific, Chicago & North Western, and the Katy.

Left: One of the last great railroad expansions in North America was the tapping of the coal deposits in the Powder River Basin in Wyoming. Over 100 miles of new track was built in the 1980s, tapping into over a dozen mines.

Opposite: The merger that didn't happen was the Santa Fe and Southern Pacific marriage. The Interstate Commerce Commission ruled against the merger, but not before some locomotives were repainted.

Right: One of the most colorful commuter operations is Tri-Rail, serving Miami, Florida. The railroad uses ten F40s from General Motors in three variations, along with double-deck passenger cars.

Below: Amtrak's standard passenger locomotive is the AEM7, built on Swedish designs. These locomotives operate between Washington and New York and on to New Haven, Connecticut (and beginning in 2000 to Boston). Amtrak operates one train a day that carries no passengers on the Northeast Corridor; a train of mail for the US Postal Service is run.

Above: New Jersey Transit operates commuter service in the New York City area, with trains terminating at Hoboken Terminal or Newark's Pennsylvania Station in New Jersey, or Pennsylvania Station in New York. ALP44 locomotives are used to power trains through the Hudson River tunnels into Manhattan.

Below: When Amtrak was shopping for new high-speed trains to operate in the Northeast Corridor, it tested two European trains brought across the Atlantic. The X2000, which operates in Sweden, departs Philadelphia on its way to Washington DC.

Above: In late 2000 Amtrak entered a new era on its electrified Northeast Corridor between Boston and Washington with the introduction of the high-speed Acela trains. Capable of attaining speeds of 135 mph, these trains have allowed Amtrak to compete with airlines in a lucrative market.

Left: The old and new on the Long Island Rail Road meet at the roundhouse in Morris Park, New York.

Opposite left: The roots of Amtrak's new Acela trains can be traced to the German Inter-City Express. Amtrak borrowed an ICE train and tested it in regular service.

Above: The Southeastern Pennsylvania Transportation Authority (SEPTA) operates commuter and light rail service in Philadelphia. A brand new AEM7 sits at Norristown, Pennsylvania, while an equally new R5-type light rail vehicle pauses overhead in a scene from 1992. Just a few years earlier, equipment that was a half-century old operated on both lines (see next page).

Left: A covered hopper car, used for carrying grain, sits under a "High Through-Put" concrete elevator at Maple Creek, Saskatchewan. The new elevators could hold as much grain as ten of the classic wooden structures that formerly dotted the Canadian prairies. Modern technology affects not only the railroads, but a whole way of life.

Right: The changing face of railroading at the dawn of the 21st Century also meant changes to the lineside industries. Wooden grain elevators in Canada were being closed, replaced by larger concrete elevators.

Opposite: A Reading "Blueliner" commuter train sits under a Red Arrow "Bullet" car (both operating for commuter agency SEPTA) at Norristown, Pennsylvania, in the late 1980s. Both would be replaced in SEPTA's modernization of the lines (see previous page).

INDEX

Picture Credits

The publishers would like to thank the following individuals and organisations
for the use of their illustrations and photographs in this book:

Black and white historical photographs (B=Bottom; C=Center; L=Left; R=Right; T=Top of the page in question):
Association of American Railroads: 10, 17, 25, 26, 27(B); Baldwin Locomotive Works: 16(R); Baltimore & Ohio Railroad Company: 12,13, 280(L), 293(R); Book Island Lines: 304(B); Burlington Northern Railway: 333; Canadian National: 40(T), 155, 169(T); Canadian Pacific Ltd: 92, 94, 121, 125(L&R), 130, 132(L), 200, 349(L); Chicago & North Western Railway: 302; Chicago Rock Island & Pacific Railroad Company: 290(L); Cincinnati Railroad Club: 102(B); DeGolyer Library: 48(T); F.G.Zahn Collection 120(T); Great Northern Railway: 169(B); H.L. Broadbelt Collection: 15(T&B), 49, 51, 59(B), 67(C&B), 83(R), 87(B), 120(B), 122(T), 170(L), 177, 181(B), 214(T&B), 215(R), 353(L), 359(B); Library of Congress/George and Helen Foster: 144(R); Minnesota Historical Society: 24, 91, 110(T), 325(R); National Archives/Brady Collection: 27(T); National Archives/Food and Drug Admin: 53; Pennsylvania Railroad: 18; RHHS Collection: 131(R); The Newberry Library: 96(L); New York Central Railroad Company: 100, 101(B), 320(L); The Oakland Museum: 29; The Pullman Company: 23; The Smithsonian Institution: 112(T), 132(T), 201(B); Union Pacific Museum Collection: 28, 31(T), 48(B), 50, 60(L), 75, 95(B), 103, 111, 112(B), 126, 127, 133, 159(T), 160(T), 168, 180, 190(L), 219(BL), 219(T), 219(BR), 274(L), 275(B), 298(L), 299(L), 303(R), 335(R), 342(L); United States Railroad Admin: 56(T); University of Washington Libraries: 60(R); US Army Signal Corps: 336(R).

Colour artwork: © Salamander Books Ltd, by: Dick Eastland; Terry Hadler; Ray Hutchins; Clifford and Wendy Meadway; David Palmer; Michael Roffe; Tiga Ltd; and W.A. Conquy.

Colour photography: The majority of colour photographs in this book were taken by the author, Steve Barry.

Colour 'memorabilia,' brochure, and poster photography: Neil Sutherland, © Salamander Books Ltd.